Tracking the Will of God

Weekly Christian motivational thoughts to help you track the plans and purposes of God

Year One

Tracking the

Will of God

Weekly Christian motivational thoughts to help you track the plans and purposes of God

Year One

Dudley Anderson

First published in Great Britain in 2021 by Dudley Anderson

ISBN 9798739175779

Dudley Anderson
E-mail: dudley@surereality.net
www. surereality.net

Dedication

To my wonderful family. I love you all so very much. Thank you for your contribution to my life and helping to provide the many experiences that have contributed to my life's track. I pray the Lord continue to bless you all and fill you daily with his sweet word as you continue to acknowledge him in all your ways.

Acknowledgements

Every time I think of the amazing people God has brought into my life I become decidedly emotional. The entries in this book are a reflection on the influence these people have had on me: family, friends, church folk, ex-colleagues and so many more. God-Tracking is not a sole endeavour. Never can we begin to assume we can face life without a generous mix of special people that God brings into our lives. God-Tracking is a process of seeking and remaining on the track of life that God has purposes for each of us, together with one another. To this end, I acknowledge the many dear people who have impacted my life. This book is an echo of God's sweet plans for my life, wrapped up with yours.

Many folks have helped me compile these accounts of my life experiences into book form. My thanks to my wife Karen, who has proofread every single e-mail version of GodTracker ever published. My thanks to daughter Kerryn and her family as well as my son Ryan and his, for their constant input into these accounts of God-Tracking. Likewise, my thanks to the dear people of my church who have, unwittingly, been the subject of many God-Tracking experiences related in this book.

My deep appreciation to Kerryn Jones for the kind permission for the use of the cover photograph.

By no means least, I want to say a massive thank you to my friend David Ettinger who has tirelessly edited each entry in this book.

By way of a final acknowledgement, I wish to thank you, dear reader, for purchasing this book. Without you a project like this would be senseless. I would love to hear your stories of tracking the plans and purposes of God. Please do make contact.

Dudley Anderson

Forward

Today's Christian has a twofold need. The first is the ability to comprehend the Bible, the eternal Word of God. The second, and very much connected with the first, is to know what to do with biblical comprehension once attaining it.

Happily, Dudley Anderson provides solutions to these crucial necessities in *God-Tracking Through the Year, Year One*. This insightful and gripping collection of 52 weekly thoughts should be a staple in every Christian's library. Dudley has an uncanny ability to choose the perfect Bible verse or passage, briefly examine it to draw out its proper meaning, and then astutely demonstrate how it fits into the life of the twenty-first century Christian. Suddenly, the grand old scriptures of millennia past come to life in new and electrifying ways.

Why electrifying? The answer is that Dudley knows how to apply the Bible to the heart of the human condition. For example, have you suffered a devastating loss – a divorce, death of a loved one, or released from your job? Dudley, with great care and compassion, displays his innate ability to find just the right Bible passage to help you cope with your current predicament. Are you battling depression? The Word of God speaks to your areas of struggle, and Dudley, with keen and tender skilfulness, not only locates those gems of divine wisdom for you, but gently shows you how to take ownership of these precious jewels.

Yet, despite the rich devotional character of this volume, *God-Trackers* also nurtures your intellect as every chapter is a Bible study in itself. We read in 2 Timothy 3:16 that "All Scripture is God-breathed." The key word here is "all," meaning *all* 66 books of the Bible. In following each devotion with suggested (and I "suggest" you read them all) verses and passages, Dudley runs the gamut from Genesis to Revelation, uniting scriptures from different sections of the Bible in perfect harmony. The fruit of Dudley's efforts will bring you clarity, wisdom, and understanding into what God is telling you. So, it's time to begin. *God-Tracking Through the Year*, *Year One* sits in your hands waiting to be explored, its treasures ready to be unearthed. The year ahead promises to be one of discovery, enrichment, and growth. Enjoy the adventure!

David Ettinger

Author of *Overcomers: 30 Stories of Triumph from the Bible*

Orlando, Florida, May 2016

Introduction

In 1996 I moved with my family from South Africa to the United Kingdom. We felt the Lord had prompted us to relocate and promised to open new opportunity for me in Christian broadcasting in the UK. We arrived on England's shores with high hopes and an expectation of great opportunity. Karen and I have always based our life's choices on Proverbs 3:6, which instructs us to acknowledge the Lord in all our ways and trust him to direct our paths. This we did, as we made a new life in England. However, for more than 12 months after we arrived, I was unemployed with no prospect of a job. During this time, the Holy Spirit made it very clear to me that, although opportunities don't always turn out as we expect, he was still definitely directing our paths. When I asked God why it seems he opens a door only to close it again, almost immediately his simple reply was, "Because, provided you acknowledge me in all your ways, you are always *on-track* with my plan for your life." Later, when opportunity eventually opened up for me to broadcast with an international radio ministry from the UK to Africa, I named my 2-hour music magazine show, *On-Track*.

On-Track was broadcast from the UK to central/southern Africa on shortwave and FM and streamed on the Internet. It was very successful with a listenership in the millions, until the station was closed in 2005. During its lifetime, On-Track solicited many favourable responses from its listeners.

One day a man wrote to me and asked me to send him my show prep by e-mail. This I did. After giving it some thought I had the idea of compiling a weekly e-mail update of my radio show prep. I called this e-mailing, GodTracker. GodTracker was favourably received by hundreds of listeners of On-Track. After some months I felt inspired to change the weekly update into a weekly e-mail devotional, which I continued to call, GodTracker. My new e-devotional was to form the bases of a ministry called, GodTracker, which is run via the website www.surereality.net

In Jeremiah 29:11 we read that the Lord knows the plans he has for us. His plans are for a good future filled with hope. As I pondered this verse, I realised that it is indeed, the Lord who knows the plans he has for us, but we do not; not until he reveals his plans to us, that is. Hence, just as an expert tracker might track a buck across the African scrub, so we need to daily track God's purposes across the plains of our lives. Tracking God's plans and purposes requires watching, listening and scrutinizing every movement, every action, word or indicator that God brings our way. This God-Tracking requires acknowledging God in all our ways and trusting him to direct our feet upon our life's track. This God-Tracking requires faith, and faith pleases God who rewards those who diligently seek him.

This book is a selection of 52 GodTracker from the many e-mail devotionals have been published over the years. Most of what you will read is based upon my own life's journey. My hope is that you will read one entry per week over the course of 12 months. As you read, pray and ask the Lord to help you discover his plans and purposes for your life. Please do read the scripture references listed in each section. These will help you get into God's Word and get God's Word into you. Remember, it takes faith to be a God-tracker and faith comes from hearing God's Word.

If you wish to know more about God-Tracking or wish to subscribe to the free weekly Christian motivational thought, GodTracker then please visit the website www. surereality.net

It is my sincere hope that you will read this Christian motivational book with a heart open to seeking the plans God has for your life. Remember, it is God who knows plans he has for you. So, time to get God-Tracking!

Week 1

GOD-TRACKING IS STEERING OUR LIVES IN LINE WITH HIS TRACKS

Proverbs 4:25

Let your eyes look straight ahead, fix your gaze directly before you.

Not too long ago I received a call on my mobile phone from my daughter, Kerryn. "Hello dad."

"Yes," I said noting the frustration in her voice. "My car won't start," she said with trepidation. Kerryn's car had broken down 20 miles away at university. She had no way of getting home. So being the pushover dad that I am, I drove out to rescue her from a fate worse than death.

When I arrived in the university carpark, I discovered there was nothing I could do to get Kerryn's car to start, and it would cost too much to hire a towing service. So, I made the decision to tow her car the 20 miles home in busy lunchtime traffic. Kerryn had never towed before so, as I linked the two cars together using a sturdy towrope, I gave her some instructions. I told her that she needed to drive the towed car, because she was not insured to drive my car. I instructed her to watch my breaking lights carefully and anticipate my every move. I told her to keep the rope taut by braking for both of us and to steer directly in line with my car as I drove in front of her. I warned her to keep a beady eye on my indicator lights and not turn left or right unless I turned left or right. I'm proud to say that, after a rather gruelling and mentally strenuous journey home, Kerryn emerged from her car triumphant after successfully negotiating a 20-mile vehicle tow.

Tracking the plans and purposes of God is a bit like steering a towed vehicle. As a follower of Jesus, I have embarked upon a journey in life that involves steering my life directly in line with my Lord's tracks, watching for his every move. I need to be sure that I keep my eyes on him at all times, carefully watching his turning indicators and his breaking lights. By his Word and by the leading of his Holy Spirit through that still small voice, I can observe which way he is leading me. If, for instance, I don't notice when he indicates a right turn, I will end up placing a great deal of strain on my tie with him and/or rip my life apart just as Kerryn would have damaged her car had she not noticed that I was turning left or right while in tow.

It is a delicate process towing a car in busy traffic and it's an equally delicate process tracking God's purposes in life. Therefore, let us make every effort to remain firmly tethered to Christ by the rope of his Word and his Spirit as we track his plans and purposes for our lives.

⇨ READ ALL ABOUT IT!
Psalm 119:105; Psalm 31:1-5; John 10:27;
2 Corinthians 4:18

Pray

"O my Lord and my guide, thank you so much that you are in charge of my life. Thank you, Lord, that you are guiding me moment by moment and helping me to track your will. I'm sorry if I have, at any time, taken my eyes off of you. Lord, I fix my gaze on you and watch for your every move and I steer my life in your ways. Help me to turn when you indicate turn and to stop when you indicate stop. Help me to never strain our relationship by going off to do things my own way. Today I tether myself to your Word and by your Spirit, I will remain in your eternal tracks. In Jesus' name. Amen."

Week 2

GOD-TRACKING IS BELIEVING YOU ARE WHERE YOU'RE MEANT TO BE

Ephesians 2:10

For we are God's workmanship, created in Christ Jesus

to do good works, which God prepared in advance.

for us to do.

"I can't understand why I didn't get the job," said Pete. "I have the required experience and qualifications. There's no reason I know of why they didn't give it to me." Pete had been unemployed for a few months and was desperate for a new job. "Did you acknowledge the Lord in this application?" I asked. "Yes," he replied. "Did you commit the application and interview to the Lord?" "Yes," again. "Then I would venture to say that this job was not *meant* for you. It simply means that the Lord has something better for you," I concluded.

One thing I have discovered is that God always means what he says and what he does. God does things on purpose! The Lord is not indecisive, as we are. The Bible tells us that God has a plan for our futures, and if we acknowledge him in all our ways, he will direct our life tracks accordingly. Sure enough, we're not off the hook in that we still need to strategize, but if we do so in prayer, by seeking his purposes first, then we will strategize according to his rules. If we acknowledge the Lord in all our ways, then he will direct the outcome.

Therefore, if you're applying for a new job or planning a new move in life, be sure to acknowledge the Lord in your plans by prayer and confession. If you're seeking plans for the future or looking for new opportunities, then seek first God's kingdom principles and his goodness. If you do this, all you could ever hope for will be added to you according to the plans *he* has for you. Believe me when I say, if you always follow this process in life, you will find yourself precisely within space and time exactly where you're *meant* to be.

So, if something doesn't work out quite like you'd hoped, you should then trust the Lord has something better for you – something *meant* for you – that will far outstrip your wildest imaginations. Remember, the Lord God watches over his Word to you to activate his plans for your life. What he promises will come about, in his time and by his design. And when it does, you will jump for joy!

 **READ ALL ABOUT IT!**
Jeremiah 29:11; Proverbs 3:5-6; Matthew 6:33;

Ephesians 3:20-21; Jeremiah 1:12; Isaiah 55:8-13

Pray

"Lord God, thank you for the plans you have for me. Thank you that all things work out for my good according to your plans. Therefore, I confess that I seek first your will and purposes in all my life's strategies. I acknowledge you in every activity, relationship and application in my life. I confess you as Lord and guide in all I set my hand to do. Thank you that you have a plan for me and that you watch over your plan to perform it in your time. Dear Lord God, come and do what you choose to do in my life. Amen."

Week 3

GOD-TRACKING IS OBSERVING HIS EVERY MINUTE DETAIL

Lamentations 3:24

I say to myself, "The Lord is my portion; therefore,
I will wait for him."

I was riveted to my television, enthralled again by the skill and sensitivity of the Kalahari Bushmen as they tracked a rhinoceros through the African bush. Pointing to the large 3-toed footprints in the sand, these expert trackers revealed how they knew not only the direction the animal was travelling but also its distance from that point. You see, the rhino had uprooted two very small seedlings with its foot as it walked through the bush. The tracker was able to calculate how far the animal was by combing its walking pace with how long it took the leaves of that small plant to wilt, given the heat of the day. "The art of tracking," said Ray Mears, the presenter of the TV documentary, "is the ability to observe every minute detail."

Jesus and his disciples had been walking the whole day in the dry heat of Judea when they entered Martha's home for a respite. Martha

9

was an excellent hostess, so she immediately set about getting supper ready. As she dashed about setting the low table and preparing the stew, she noticed her sister, Mary, who shared the house with her, sitting at Jesus' feet, listening intently to his every Word. "Lord, don't you care that my sister has left me to do the work by myself? Tell her to help me!" said Martha with indignation. "Martha, Martha," the Lord answered. "You are worried and upset about many things, but only one thing is needed. Mary has chosen what is better, and it will not be taken away from her."

If you're anything like I am then I'm sure every time you read this story you feel an affinity with Martha. After all, she was only giving her all to serve her Lord. Isn't this something we should aspire to as God-trackers? And yes, indeed, it certainly is correct and good to do all our hand finds to do with all our might as unto the Lord. However, Jesus was quick to point out to Martha that she was so busy getting things together for the *work of the Lord* that she was missing the *Lord of the work*. In her God-Tracking, Martha was running frantically about gaining an overview of who Jesus was while it was Mary who was sitting quietly at his feet, keeping her eyes on Jesus and observing every minute detail of his movements.

⇨ **READ ALL ABOUT IT!**
Luke 10:40-42; Hebrews 12:2

Pray

"Dear Lord, I want to take a moment to thank you for all you have given me including my responsibilities at work, at home and at church. However, like Martha, I often get so caught up with the work to be done that I neglect the smaller more important details in tracking your purposes. In you all things in my life hold together; in you I live and move and have my being so I realise now that it's very foolish to be drawn away from your presence by taking my eyes off you. Today I choose to walk with you and listen to your voice, alone. I choose to watch for your minute moves along the way. Like a tracker tracking his prey through the African scrub, help me to observe every detail of your will for my life. Amen."

Week 4

GOD-TRACKING IS WALKING IN THE FOOTSTEPS OF JESUS, EVEN ON WATER

Matthew 14:31

Immediately Jesus reached out his hand and caught him. "You of little faith," he said, "why did you doubt?"

The concept of God-Tracking is based upon the understanding that God has a deliberate, exclusive, designer purpose for our lives. It has been said that God works in mysterious ways to perform his wonders. I agree. However, what sometimes appears mysterious to us is pure logic to God. As the scripture tells us, "For the foolishness of God is wiser than man's wisdom." Therefore, as we seek to track God's unique plans for our lives, we need to operate not according our own human logic but according to the logic of faith in God's often mysterious ways.

Late one stormy night out on Lake Tiberias, Jesus' disciples were straining at the oars to keep their small boat upright. The wind was howling through the mast and rigging. The others were shouting commands to each other, but Peter was silently wondering why Jesus had sent them on ahead in the boat. Surely, he knew there was a storm brewing? Didn't he care if they perished? What was his purpose in all this? Just then Peter heard Thomas shriek above the wind, "Out there! It's a ghost!" Peter looked up, squinting through the rain. Sure enough, there was a figure standing out there standing *on* the water! They all began to panic, but then heard a familiar voice reassuring them who it was. "Lord, if it's you," Peter cried, "tell me to come to you on the water." Jesus said, "Come." Peter cautiously stepped out of the boat onto the raging lake. He was standing – standing *on* the water! Peter took one step, two. He was literally walking on the water – walking in the footsteps of Jesus. Suddenly, Peter took his eyes off his Lord and looked at the waves around him. He lost his faith and began to sink until Jesus reached out and rescued him.

It could be that you are facing a new prospect today. Perhaps you're in the process of changing jobs or hearing the call of God to take a leap of faith into fulltime Christian ministry. You may be facing a new business move into a venture that scares you witless and you're wondering, as might Peter have, can God really be in all this? God-Tracking requires that we continuously acknowledge God in all our ways and not trust in our own logic, but rather in God's wisdom. God-Tracking requires us to trust the Holy Spirit to guide us according to his deliberate, exclusive, designer purpose for our lives. And God-Tracking requires that we constantly keep our eyes on Jesus, the author of life.

So, if you're sitting in a sinking boat today wondering why the Lord sent you out into the storm in the first place, take that step of faith out of the boat and walk where Jesus is walking, even if it's on water!

⇨ READ ALL ABOUT IT!

Isaiah 55:6-13; 1 Corinthians 1:18-31;
Matthew 14:22-33

Pray

"Dear Lord, I am afraid to take that step out of the boat, even when I know it's you out there on the water. Sometimes your plans for my life appear mysterious. However, I know you have good reasons for doing the things you are doing in my life. So, I repent of my little faith and commit my future to you. I acknowledge you in all my ways and trust you will direct my paths according to your ways. Help me to take that plunge; help me to make this move and step out of the boat in faith and not in human reason. Thank you that you have a deliberate, exclusive, designer purpose for my life. I accept your purpose by faith. Help me to walk in it. Amen."

15

Week 5

GOD-TRACKING IS GIVING NO LESS
THAN YOUR BEST FOR HIM

Colossians 3:17

And whatever you do, whether in word or deed, do it all in the name of the Lord Jesus, giving thanks to God the Father through him

It was Friday afternoon and my colleagues had the wisdom to give me a wide berth. I'd been working on a radio documentary for several weeks collecting material, doing interviews and writing scripts. I was busy with the final edit with the project due by Monday and was a little frayed around the edges. Listening carefully to every nuance of the recordings, I fine-tuned the edit over and over again until I was mostly satisfied with it. Although I could still hear the little mistakes, I reached the point where there was nothing more I could do to improve the production. I had to let it go. I'd done my best.

Dear God-tracker, none of us can be the best at everything we do but we can do our best at what we do, do. Confused? Let me explain. As you and I track God's purposes, by his grace, he calls us to his service and opens doors for us to produce the *product* of our lives.

That *product* is the result of everything we set our hands to do. It may be a song sung at church or a school project or an art piece or an essay. It may be clearing tables at a coffee shop or teaching life skills to a class of special-needs children. Your life's *product* could be keeping books for a small business or fixing cars as a motor mechanic. It could be that your life's *product* is building houses, cleaning offices, driving a taxi or performing brain surgery. Whatever it is you are called to do – whatever your life's *product* – you need to strive for excellence. And to me, this is excellence: "Whatever your hand finds to do, do it with *all your might!*"

You see, God doesn't expect you to be more than you are, but he does expect you to be *all* that you are. The Bible tells us that we should always be abounding in the work of the Lord, knowing that in the Lord our labour is not in vain and whatever we do in life we should do it in the name of Jesus. Therefore, whatever your hand finds to do it with all your heart, as unto Jesus.

 **READ ALL ABOUT IT!**
Ecclesiastes 9:10; 1 Corinthians 15:58

Pray

"Father God help me to do all I do to the best of my ability. Thank you for giving me the skills to do my job and to serve you. I choose

to give it all I've got and to do all I do as unto you, my Lord. I know that your eyes are on everything I do, therefore, I don't need to work to be recognised by man. Help me at my work O Lord, to do it with all my might. Sometimes it's tough and sometimes I feel as though it's all for nothing, but I know that in you, nothing is in vain. I give you the product of my life. Amen."

Week 6

GOD-TRACKING IS MAKING A POINT OF GRACE

2 Corinthians 5:21

God made him who had no sin to be sin for us, so that in him we might become the righteousness of God.

A man arrives at the pearly gates. Peter says, "Here's how it works. You need 100 points to make it into heaven. You tell me all the good things you've done, and I give you a certain number of points for each item, depending on how good it was. When you reach 100 points, you get in."

"Okay," the man says eyeing the rack of designer halos on the other side of the gate. "First off, I attended church every single Sunday."

"That's good," says St. Peter, "that's worth two points."

"Two points?" says the man. "Well... er... I always gave 10% of all my earnings to the church. Does that count?"

"Hmm, let's see," answers Peter, "that's worth another 2 points. Did you do anything else?"

"Two points!? Well, how about this: I started a soup kitchen in my city and worked in a shelter for the homeless."

"Fantastic, that's certainly worth another point," says Peter. The man ponders for a moment and then adds, "And I was married to the same woman for 50 years and never cheated on her, even in my heart."

"That's wonderful. Let's see now. That's worth another… three points!"

"Only three points!!" the man cries, "At this rate the only way I'll ever get into heaven is by the grace of God!"

"At last," replies Peter. "Come on in!"

You may smile, but isn't it funny how we often think we can store up brownie points with God? We do all the right things, like giving to disaster funds, helping our neighbours and even attending a few church meetings or Bible studies. BY this we think we'll be okay on "D"-day when that final trumpet sounds and we face the Judge. After all, we were born into a good Christian home, believed in God all our lives and even called Jesus, Lord.

However, listen to what Jesus once said: "Not everyone who says to me, 'Lord, Lord,' will enter the kingdom of heaven, but only he who does the will of my Father who is in heaven," and again, "Why do you call me, 'Lord, Lord,' and do not do what I say?" You see, dear God-tracker, it's not how many credits we earn by good works and sweet talk that makes us right with God, it's only by following God's will and his Word. And God's Word tells us that it is his will to justify by grace through faith alone!

Jesus also said things like: "For I tell you that unless your righteousness surpasses that of the Pharisees and the teachers of the law, you will certainly not enter the kingdom of heaven." The Pharisees of Jesus' day believed that their righteousness gave them credit with God. But all the good works in all the world will never be good enough to match God's righteousness! Only Christ's good works are good enough for God and only faith in Christ's good work on the cross accredits us with righteousness. When he died Jesus became sin for us so that, in him, we might become the righteousness of God. Therefore, it is only *in Christ* that your and my righteousness can surpass that of the Pharisees!

And that's God's grace! All that remains is for you to take Jesus at his word, humbly accept God's grace by faith and decide to track his will for the rest of your life. Good works are man's way but grace is God's way.

⇨ **READ ALL ABOUT IT!**

Matthew 7:21-23; Luke 6:46-49; Romans 3:27-28;
Matthew 5:20; 2 Corinthians 5:21

Pray

"Oh God, I confess that I have been trying to earn good points to be right with you. I'm very sorry and I admit that I was wrong. There is nothing I can do that will be good enough to gain access to heaven except to humble myself and come to you through Jesus, just as I am. This I do now, O Lord. I lay down my good works and admit to my sin. I repent of all that I have done that has grieved you. I am weary of doing good works and come to you, O Jesus, to find rest from my own efforts. Thank you for your grace. Thank you for dying in my place and taking my sin at Calvary so that I can be made righteous before God by your goodness and sacrifice, and not my own efforts. I rest in your grace, Lord. Amen."

Week 7

GOD-TRACKING IS GIVING GOD SPACE TO FULFIL HIS WORD IN YOUR LIFE

Jeremiah 1:12

The LORD said to me, "You have seen correctly, for I am watching to see that my word is fulfilled."

King David's men had just returned from striking the Philistines at Gezer. The Lord had helped him in this mighty and victorious campaign against his enemy. David was pleased. To celebrate and give thanks to the Lord, he calls for the Ark of the Covenant to be brought up from the house of Abinadab. Abinadab and his sons, Uzzah and Ahio, load it up on a cart and set off. Shortly after they set off the oxen pulling the cart stumble and the Ark of the Covenant begins to fall to the ground. Uzzah makes a grab for it to steady it, but in his haste forgets the command of God that no one could touch the Ark of the Covenant, or they will die. Instantly he is struck down.

Do you think it is unfair that Uzzah died just because he tried to protect the Ark of the Covenant from falling? Surely it would've fallen and shattered into pieces... or would it have? You see, God had given Moses a commandment to forbid anyone from touching the Ark because of its holiness. This was the same God who, by his Word, had commanded the universe into being. When God speaks no man can supplement his word or detract from it. God is very capable of watching over his own word to fulfil it. If this is true then, even if the Ark had fallen, it would have been safe. The Ark contained the Ten Commandments that God gave Moses on Mount Sinai and, in his flippancy, Uzzah had paid the price of assuming he could watch over God's Word to safeguard it.

In the same way, the Lord is watching over his Word in your life to safeguard his purposes for you. He does have a plan for you; a plan to prosper you and not to harm you. There is, indeed, hope for the situation you face today. If you seek the Lord with all your heart you will discover he has plans to restore your fortunes and make way for your future. His Word has promised health to your flesh and peace to your soul. The Bible says that just as the rain and the snow come down from heaven and do not evaporate back to it without watering the earth and making it bud and flourish, so is the Word that goes out from his mouth; It will not return to him empty but will accomplish what he desires and achieve the purpose for which he sent it. Your God is more than capable of accomplishing all the plans and purposes he has for you, with success and blessing. So, resist the temptation of reaching out in your own strength in a feeble attempt to guide God's promises to you. Instead, rest in the security that he is watching over his Word to you, even when it seems you're falling.

⟹ **READ ALL ABOUT IT!**
2 Samuel 6:1-8; Jeremiah 1:11-12;
Isaiah 55:10-11

Pray

"Thank you, my Lord, for all your promises to me. Thank you that you have given me your word that you will direct my purposes if I continue to acknowledge you in all I do. Thank you that you will meet all my needs according to your riches in Christ and provide me with peace from my anxieties as I pray with thanksgiving. Thank you for my health; for the people who love me and for the hope of a blessed future. I am sorry for taking you for granted and for becoming flippant about your word. Forgive me for trying to make your promises come about by my own efforts. Today I realise that you are able to watch over your word and your purposes in my life far, far better than I could ever do. Praise you Father that your promises are always yes, in Jesus. Amen!"

Week 8

GOD-TRACKING IS TRUSTING GOD TO WORK ALL THINGS OUT FOR YOUR GOOD

2 Corinthians 9:8

And God is able to make all grace abound to you, so that in all things at all times, having all that you need, you will abound in every good work.

Karen and I had once committed ourselves to a small fellowship group that met close to our new home. We were very happy there and had dreams for the future of our group. However, just a few short months after we had settled in our leader, announced that he was merging our group with another small church that met not too far from where we were meeting.

All went well for a couple of years as we adjusted to the new style and format. Our new pastor was a likable guy and I soon found myself confiding in him about the call to ministry I had sensed upon my life since leaving school. He listened with intent as I poured out my heart about the current condition of my career in the IT industry and my desire to serve God fulltime. When I'd finished speaking, he looked at me with a twinkle in his eye and said, "Dudley, I believe God is calling you to leave your job and go to Bible College." I liked what I heard and, after much prayer and discussion, Karen and I agreed that it was time to take the plunge.

My new pastor was initially most supportive of my move and I was led to believe that there was promise of someday joining him in overseeing this growing church. However, not too long after I'd given up my job and went to study for the ministry, my pastor called me into his office and accused me of wanting to, "split the church." I was flabbergasted! I could not believe what I was hearing and asked him to repeat what he said. The furthest thing from my mind was to split this church that I had grown to love and to jeopardise my future in the ministry. Sadly, one thing led to the next and eventually Karen and I were forced to resign.

There I was, studying for the ministry with no church covering or hope for the future. How could anything good come of this? Despair crept in. It was then that an old friend invited us to visit his church. We went along and liked what we found. Eventually we committed ourselves to our new church. The pastor was a man of integrity who advised me to continue my studies and trust God to work out all the details, as only he can. He said, "Dudley, God has a plan for all our lives. If he has called you then he will direct you accordingly. And remember," he added, "all things eventually work together for our good, in Christ."

The following years would prove to be the most gruelling of our lives. Karen and I went through financial crises, marital dilemma and intense personal depression. If we were not under the counsel of our new pastor at this time, I firmly believe I would not be writing to you today. He and his lovely wife stood by Karen and me through thick and thin and held up our arms in the battle. These God-fearing leaders invested in us. They sought the Lord on our behalf; they disciplined me; they supported me in my studies and most importantly, they loved Karen and me. I don't know what I would have done without them both.

Dear God-tracker, God knows where you are in the fight of life right now. He loves you and he will rescue you. Though your hopes and dreams may seem to be crumbling, provided you continue to acknowledge the Lord in all you do and trust him to direct your paths, then all things will work out for your good. Even though Satan may be shooting his fiery darts of doubt and despair at you and attacking you through sickness or anxiety, raise your shield of faith and stand firm in the plans God has for you! When those you trust let you down, remember that he will never leave nor forsake you.

Your destiny may appear to be in ruins but remind yourself that you walk by faith and not by sight.

READ ALL ABOUT IT!
Jeremiah 29:11; Proverbs 3:5-6; Romans 8:26-30

Pray

"O Lord, I'm so confused. It seems like my life is falling apart around me. People are letting me down and all that I have dreamed about is crumbling in front of my eyes. I face illness, financial crises and confusion at every turn. Lord, I'm sorry if I have taken my eyes off of you and your purposes for me. Thank you so much for your grace – it's only by your grace that I face tomorrow with any hope at all. Indeed, thank you for my difficult times, because they make me stronger in you. Despite what I see going on around me I believe you are in it all, Lord. You know my beginning from my end and you know the things that work for my good. I believe that you will bring the right people into my life to help me achieve my dreams. So, I acknowledge you Lord my God in all I am, all I do and in every relationship I have. I trust you to direct my paths and bring good out of every adverse situation. Help me abound in every good work for your sake. Amen."

Week 9

GOD-TRACKING IS NURTURING IN THE VISION HE HAS GIVEN YOU, DESPITE SEEMING FAILURES

Hebrews 10:36

You need to persevere so that when you have done the will of God, you will receive what he has promised.

I have a lovely white orchid plant growing in a pot on my bathroom windowsill. It is a very rewarding sight and fills the room with cheer. Currently, it's boasting 33 blossoms, but it's not always been this prolific. When I purchased the plant, it had four or five blooms, but after they died off it stood dormant for a very long time. I faithfully watered its roots and moistened its leaves, but to no avail. But then one winter I noticed little buds appearing between its leaves. These buds grew and grew until two longs stems produced the display I'm now enjoying so much. I must admit there were times I thought I should just get rid of the orchid but, thankfully, I persevered in my nurture until I was rewarded for my faithfulness.

A story is told of young William Wilberforce, who was most discouraged one night in the early 1790s after another defeat in his 10-year battle against the slave trade in England. Tired and frustrated, he opened his Bible to read. As he did, a small piece of paper dropped out. It was a letter written by his friend John Wesley shortly before his death. Wilberforce read it again: "Unless God has raised you up for this very thing, you will be worn out by the opposition of men and devils. But if God be for you, who can be against you? Are all of them together stronger than God? Oh, be not weary of well-doing. Go on in the name of God, and in the power of His might."

Two accounts of endurance (though I'll admit the latter is a little more honourable than the first). However, in both the cases it was the nurture of a vision that produced the fruit. If I had given up watering my favourite pot plant, it would have died off and never produced the reward it now gives. If Wilberforce had given up plying parliament to abolish slavery, we'd be living in a very different world today. Faithful endurance continues to water the vision in faith that God will produce the fruit, as he alone can.

⇨ **READ ALL ABOUT IT!**
Hebrews 10:19-23; Romans 8:31-32; Romans 5:1-5;
James 1:2-7; Colossians 3:23-24

Pray

"Dear Lord, I admit, I'm weary of working at this vision. It seems that I see no fruit to my labour. And yet I realise that I need to faithfully continue nurturing it with all my might. I know you have given me this vision; you have called me to do this work for you at such a time as this. Help me to see beyond these seeming failures to the success you've promised. Help me to continue watering this vision by your inspiration, as I would a flowering plant without blossoms, until I reap the reward you bring. I realise that it may take a long time to bloom, O Lord, but I choose to be faithful at what you have called me to do. If you are for me, who can be against me? I will continue to go on in the name of God, and in the power of His might. Jesus, you are my very great reward. Amen."

Week 10

GOD-TRACKING IS BEING TOTALLY SOLD OUT FOR CHRIST

Romans 12:11

Never be lacking in zeal, but keep your spiritual fervour, serving the Lord.

The Internet is an amazing resource. It has transformed the world into a village. Through it I have enjoyed the privilege of getting to know some wonderful people in communities that I would never have otherwise been able to discover. One such person was a pastor called Rashid Emmanuel, from a church in Pakistan. A passionate man of God, Rashid pastored his church on the foundation of the Gospel of our Lord Jesus. Always willing to stand up for the truth of the message of Christ, Rashid would unashamedly preach God's word with zeal in a community averse to Christianity. I deeply admired him as a man sold out for Christ. Unfortunately, Rashid and his brother Sajid were arrested and tried for blasphemy charges against Islam. Sadly, one Monday afternoon after being acquitted of these charges Rashid Emmanuel, just 36, and his younger brother

Sajid, 30, were maliciously gunned down on the steps outside as they left the courtroom as in Faisalabad.

Jesus said, "Whoever finds his life will lose it, and whoever loses his life for my sake will find it." He then went on to teach a parable about the Kingdom of God saying, "The kingdom of heaven is like a merchant looking for fine pearls. When he found one of great value, he went away and sold everything he had and bought it." God's Kingdom – that is, salvation and life by the Holy Spirit – is an extremely valuable commodity. Unlike Rashid Emmanuel I may never be called to actually give my life for God's Kingdom but it is my desire to surrender my daily living to serve the Lord my God. I desire to be totally committed to my cause just as Jesus was to his and, indeed, as Rashid was to his. And if the devil should ever come to my store one day looking to buy a part of me, I want him to find a sign across my counter saying, "TOTALLY SOLD OUT TO JESUS!"

Walking with God requires total surrender to his plans. Surrender is defined as "the cessation of struggle or ceasing the resistance of the influence of another". When you surrender, you lay down your arms; you submit, yield and give up. Jesus said, "If anyone would come after me, he must deny himself and take up his cross and follow me." Being a God-tracker, therefore, requires fervent surrender. Jesus once said to the Apostle John that he wishes we would be either cold or hot, but if we are lukewarm, he will spew us from his mouth. Tracking God's plans and purposes for life requires the need to be prepared to live in that *hot zone*. Like Rashid Emmanuel – like Jesus Christ himself – let's be willing to sell all we have for a treasure so great that the world itself could not contain it.

⇨ READ ALL ABOUT IT!
Matthew 10:39; Matthew 13:45-46; Matthew 16:24;
Revelation 3:16

Pray

"Dear Lord, thank you for the great heroes of our faith who are willing to stand for the truth of the gospel and lay their lives down for the kingdom of God. I pray today for the family and church of Rashid and Sajid Emmanuel in Pakistan, that you will strengthen them and protect them. Lord, help me to learn from the thousands like Rashid who are willing to give it all up for Jesus. Your kingdom is of great worth because you are worthy O God to receive all praise and glory. Today I ask that you help me to be totally sold out for Jesus as he was for me on the cross. Jesus, you said that in this world we would have trouble but to take heart, because you have overcome the world. When I consider your strength, O Lord, I am strengthened. Therefore, I choose to live in the red-hot zone,

fervently surrendered to God and filled with your Spirit. In you I do not grow weary or lose heart. Amen."

Week 11

GOD-TRACKING IS BRAVELY TRACKING HIS PLANS WHEREVER THEY MAY LEAD

Psalm 138:3

When I called, you answered me; you made me bold and stout-hearted.

God-Tracking is based on the idea that, if God has plans for you – plans for a hope and a future – then you need to set your face toward seeking and tracking his plans no matter where they may lead you. God is sovereign, his will is supreme and his purposes are just. Therefore, as you track God's plans for a hope and a future, you need to be willing to submit to his purposes and remain within his will. But here's the thing: whatever God's plans turn out to be and wherever you may find yourself as you track his will, you will never be abandoned by his grace and fatherly care.

I recently heard a moving story of a pastor of a small church in Kazakhstan. His church was opposite a mosque with a congregation in the thousands. One day the imam of the mosque summonsed the pastor and his small church to appear before him and his followers.

The pastor and his flock obliged. Standing up before them, the imam declared, "We instruct you to close your church and convert to Islam. If you do not deny Jesus, then we will kill you all." There was silence in the mosque as the pastor quietly raised his hands and said, "You may kill our bodies, but our souls will always be safe in Christ our Lord. And I will never, never deny Jesus my Lord and Saviour." Slowly the rest of the humble church group raised their hands and echoed their leader's sentiment. A buzz broke out in the mosque as the people waited for the imam's response. After a long pause he said, "Because of your bold commitment to your belief I have decided to let you all return home." A few days later the imam offered an apology to the pastor and his congregation.

Tracking God's plans may often lead you into situations beyond your control. However, that's not a bad place to be. As you boldly continue to acknowledge the Lordship of Christ and walk according to God's will (wherever it may lead you), remember that he will direct your paths and control your circumstances. You may never face physical persecution for your faith, as this pastor in Kazakhstan did, but, in this world, you will certainly be faced with the temptation to compromise your faith or your moral integrity. When this happens remember to stand strong in Christ and bravely praise God's name in the face of the gods of this world. Whatever situation you may face in this world; whatever the devil levels at you, know this:

nothing will separate you from the love of God that is Christ Jesus! Your Lord will make you bold and stout-hearted as you humbly track his plans and purposes in life.

⇨ READ ALL ABOUT IT!
Jeremiah 29:11; Deuteronomy 31:6; Psalm 138;
Romans 8:31-39

Pray

"O most holy God, I know that your will for my life is supreme. Help me to always stay on-track with your will and your plans. Thank you that you will never abandon me. I know that I can trust in your grace and power to get me through every adverse situation that I may find myself in. Lord, I reaffirm that I acknowledge you in all my ways and I trust you to direct my paths however they may appear to me. I know that all things work out good in the end, as you direct my ways. I submit my life and my future to your plans for me. In Jesus' name. Amen."

Week 12

GOD-TRACKING IS BOLDLY GOING WHERE YOU'VE NEVER BEEN BEFORE

Deuteronomy 31:6

Be strong and courageous. Do not fear or be in dread of them, for it is the Lord your God who goes with you. He will not leave you or forsake you."

When I was about 12-years old, a cousin showed me a few chords on an old guitar. I eagerly learned the three-chord wonder, *I'm on the Top of the World*, in the key of A. However, because I didn't have a guitar of my own, I soon lost interest. About 4 years later a friend of my brother gave me a beat-up buzzing old guitar that was impossible to tune. I loved that old thing and was motivated again to give music another bash. I taught myself a few more chords and was encouraged to play along with my youth leader during sing-a-longs at youth-group meetings. Soon, with a new 12-string under my arm, I found myself leading a few choruses before the evening service at church. Even so, I had no deep-seated aspiration to become the next

Phil Keaggy of the Christian music world and yet… God had plans for me.

I was soon to find the girl of my dreams and we settled in a city away from home. After 3 months we found a good little church a few minutes' drive from our new inner-city apartment. Over tea at the end of the service one Sunday morning it was discovered that I and a friend, who had come to church with me, were guitarists.

"Would you play for us next Sunday," was the prompt request.

"Next Sunday!?"

"Yes, our previous worship leader left two weeks ago and we've been praying that the Lord would soon send us a new one. And he has!" I was flabbergasted. By now I had indeed added a few new chords to my repertoire, but I was practically not ready to take to the stage of a new church in front of 150 people, leading praise and worship. And yet, I had a deep sense that the Lord was doing what he has always done in my life – plunging me into the deep end and saying, "Do not be dismayed, I am always with you. Just swim!"

In the beginning of the book of Joshua we read of how the Lord gave Joshua a command to lead his people across the raging Jordan River into the new Promised Land. Up till that point, ol' Josh was only Moses' sidekick Indeed, he was a brave warrior but had no experience of leading a nation to colonise a new territory, let alone be their spiritual oversight. Through Moses, God commanded Joshua to conquer Jericho and every city of Canaan. Moses had also instructed Joshua to be the judge of the people, teaching and implementing the Law of God. What a task! Joshua found himself in the deep end with the words, "Only be strong and courageous," ringing in his ears.

Dear God-tracker, if you continue to acknowledge the Lord in all your ways; if you continue to walk by faith and not by sight and if you keep your eyes on Jesus the author and perfecter of your faith, then God will direct your paths according to his will. Remember, his grace is sufficient to equip you for his every purpose. Therefore, don't be surprised the next time you find yourself treading water in the great schemes of life. Just remember he is with you always even in the deep end.

 **READ ALL ABOUT IT!**
Joshua 1-4; 2 Corinthians 12:9-10

Pray

"Father God I know my life is wrapped up in your will, but sometimes I feel completely unqualified to do the things you call me to do. Help me to walk confidently, by your grace, in your will at all times. I accept your plans for my life even when I'm seemingly plunged into the deep end. Sometimes I find myself floundering,

trying to keep head above the waves. And yet, I know you are always with me and your purposes will prevail in my life. Lord, I submit my skills and talents to you; do with them what you will. I continue to acknowledge you and trust you to direct my paths as I keep my eyes on Jesus. Amen."

Week 13

GOD-TRACKING IS ALLOWING HIM TO DIRECT THE STORY OF YOUR LIFE

Psalm 119:35

Direct me in the path of your commands, for there I find delight.

I once played as an extra in a small part in a film. The production employed several professional actors, a large crew and an even larger cast of extras. This company must have been a handful to direct. In the one and only scene in which I appeared I was given instructions to walk across an open field with a bunch of other extras while the main actors were instructed to do whatever it was that they were to do.

The director was the typical character that you'd always imagined a film director to be large loudhailer in hand, hollering commands to everyone on set. He also had a team of runners on standby that would dart in and out of props and actors carrying out his instructions. At the director's side sat the continuity girl who, with clipboard in hand, kept tabs of every actor's and every extra's position and expression, while the cameras were rolling. The continuity girl acted on behalf of the director, maintaining every aspect of the shape and form that was playing out in the scene before him. To me it seemed as though the director was omnipresent and omniscient. Every crew member, actor, and extra kept his eyes and ears tuned to the director's voice so that he would not miss his mark.

Dear God-tracker, the Lord our God is the Director in this production we call life. Just as the crew and cast of a film set follow their director's instructions, so too we need to explicitly follow God's instructions as we seek to play out his purposes. And our Director is truly omnipresent and omniscient as well as omnipotent. Like the continuity girl, the Holy Spirit is aware of every gesture, every move and every expression of our lives and has the power to give our lives meaning. Like the runners, God's angels are his messengers running in and out of our circumstances carrying out his commands. On the movie set, the whole company fixes its eyes on the director and follows his directions. Likewise, on the stage of your life you too need to fix your eyes on Jesus, the author the Director of your faith.

So, continue to acknowledge the Lord God in all your ways and be sure that, by his Word and through his Spirit, he will produce a box-office extravaganza of your life!

 **READ ALL ABOUT IT!**
Psalm 33:6-16; Psalm 57:2; Proverbs 16:1-4

Pray:

"O my Lord, I'm sorry for trying to do things my way. I realise now that you are the only one who can direct my life. I want to let go of my own ideas and turn my life over to your purposes. I've cluttered up my pathway so much that I'm tripping with every step I take. Help me to hear your voice; help me to watch for your hand at work and be ready to act out your every command. Lord I choose to step out in faith and put my trust in your plans for my life. Jesus, I fix my eyes on you so that I may follow your script for my life. Direct me according to your purposes, Lord. Amen."

Week 14

GOD-TRACKING IS ALWAYS KNOWING THAT GOD KNOWS IT ALL

Psalm 139:3

You discern my going out and my lying down; you are familiar with all my ways.

In 1985 an American singer-songwriter, Julie Gold, was working as a secretary when she wrote a song that Bette Midler took to number one on the Adult Contemporary chart in 1990. The song talks about how peaceful the world would look from far away and has the refrain, "God is watching us, God is watching us, God is watching us from a distance." It's a nice song but I ask, *is God watching from a distance?!*

Several years ago, I was going through a particularly difficult time. I was overworked, underpaid and totally stressed out. You know the feeling, when it seems everyone is ganging up on you (though they're not really) and it feels as though you have no one to talk to. In the middle of my predicament, my wife and I were invited to a meeting where a lady with the gift of prophecy was ministering.

It was a small group, so after her talk she spent a few minutes praying over individuals. When she came to me the Lord gave her a word of knowledge upon which she proceeded to describe all I was going through at that time, in detail. You must understand that I had not met this woman before that night and I'd not had any conversation with her prior to this moment. Added to this was the fact that no one else in that group, except my wife, knew of my situation. I can safely say that the Holy Spirit had indeed given this minister the information she was now sharing with me. At that very moment I realised something quite profound. I realised because she knew what I was going through, I knew, God knew!

Dear God-tracker, the Lord your God is not watching you from a distance; he is as close to you as your own breath. In fact, God knows more about you than you know yourself, because he knows your future. And God knows what's going on in your life at this exact moment. The Scriptures remind us to acknowledge him in every aspect of our lives and then to trust that he will direct the outcome according to his purposes. And his purposes are always good! If you continue to acknowledge the Lord in all your ways, he will chart your paths and tell you where to stop and rest. He knows precisely where you are in life at every moment. So, come to Jesus today and rest in his love, in his care, and in his purposes.

⇨ READ ALL ABOUT IT!

1 Corinthians 12:1-11; Psalm 139; Psalm 121; Proverbs 3:5-6; Romans 8:28; Matthew 11:28-30

Pray

"O my Lord, thank you so much that you know all about what I am going through at this time. Sometimes it seems no one cares but I know that you care, so I cast my cares upon you. I know you are powerful and loving and that you contain all I will ever need to get through these difficulties. Therefore, I rest in your love, power and provision in the knowledge that you always know precisely where I am on this track of life. Thank you, Jesus. Amen."

Week 15

GOD-TRACKING IS BELIEVING IN GOD'S GOODNESS WITH REAL FAITH

Matthew 21:21

And Jesus answered them, "Truly, I say to you, if you have faith and do not doubt, you will not only do what has been done to the fig tree, but even if you say to this mountain, 'Be taken up and thrown into the sea', it will happen.

Peter Bohler once said to John Wesley, "Preach faith till you have it; and then, because you have it, preach faith." Sadly, the word "faith" these days has developed many connotations. Nowadays, we hear self-improvement motivational speakers telling us to have faith in ourselves. Then there are those multi-faith advocates telling us that all faiths lead to the same end. In fact, we have replaced the word "religions" with the word "faiths" to refer to the array of belief systems in the world. There is even a clothing brand called, Faith. And yet, the one thing we read that disappointed Jesus Christ the most was when he encountered people of *little* faith.

The Bible tells us that faith is the confidence in things hoped for and being certain of a life unseen. It says that without faith it is impossible to please God, because anyone who comes to him must believe that he exists and that he rewards those who earnestly seek him. Only by faith can we look beyond the barriers we encounter in life and realise God's provision.

One night, with some of his disciples sleeping just yards from him, Jesus was sitting flat in the dirt of a garden near an olive tree, weeping before his Father. He said, "Father, if it's your will please may this cup pass from me... Oh Abba..." Jesus sinks His head into His hands as drops of blood from burst capillaries in his skin, mixed with His sweat, dampen His fingers. He knows he's facing the cross and an agonizing death. Slowly Jesus raises His head and, by faith, sighs, "Abba, not what I want but your will be done." Suddenly the power of the Son of God that he is surges through His body and Jesus looks beyond the cross and sees himself raised from the dead, exalted to God's right hand and glorified as King of kings!

The Bible says, "Let us fix our eyes on Jesus, the author and perfecter of our faith, who for the joy set before him endured the cross, scorning its shame, and sat down at the right hand of the throne of God." By Christ's example of faith in God, take your eyes off the pain in your body and fix them on God's healing power. By faith, take your eyes off that debt or joblessness that you face and see

God's provision for all that you need. Don't focus on the problems in your marriage but, with faith in God, look to the Lover of your soul and, with a softened heart, trust the only One who can reunite you in His love. Today, dear friend, open your heart to God's forgiveness, by faith, and don't rely on your own inadequate good works to make you right before the Lord. Take Christ's example and by faith in God, look through the hopelessness of your problems and know that God already has a blessed and prosperous future planned for you. Faith is more than simply a synonym for religion or a buzz word for self-improvement. Put real faith in Christ today and believe that He does have a beautiful plan for your tomorrow.

⇨ READ ALL ABOUT IT!
Hebrews 11; Hebrews 12:1-3; Jeremiah 29:11

Pray

"Dear Lord, I realise now that real faith is the substance of things I hope for in life. Today I ask your forgiveness for my lack of faith. I step out assured and lay claim to your word with the sheer confidence that you will do what you have promised to do. And Lord, I confess that you have promised to meet all my needs according to your glorious riches in Jesus. I confess, by faith, that you will heal my body and heal my relationships that you may be glorified. I

believe that you do have a plan for my life and in faith I look beyond the barriers in front of me and see myself today as you see me tomorrow. Thank you, Lord. Amen."

Week 16

GOD-TRACKING IS RESTING IN THE EFFORT OF FAITH, IN GOD'S GRACE

Matthew 11:28

Come to me, all you who are weary and burdened, and I will give you rest.

"I am trying so hard," said my young colleague on the coach to church one Sunday morning. "I've already prayed *the* prayer and I'm attending church, but it's just so tough *trying* to be born again!" We were talking about how to become a Christian. I'd quoted Jesus' words to Nicodemus, "No one can see the kingdom of God unless he is born again." Jesus was, of course, talking about how, if we desired to know God's forgiveness and the promise of heaven, we need to be born of the Spirit. That is, because all of us are spiritually dead in sin, we need to be spiritually born, or *born again*, in order to know new life in Jesus. My friend knew the theory but she was attempting to get born again by working hard at being a good person. Truth be told, that's an impossible feat! We can only be born again and made right before God by God's grace through faith. It's the simplest thing in the world: in faith, admit and turn from sin, confess Jesus as Lord and believe that he died and rose again. Through Jesus, God's grace has saved us all from sin and our faith in his work of grace is all that is required for salvation. If my colleague had simply done this, I believe she would have experienced spiritual new birth with no effort of her own.

The Bible tells us we are saved by God's effort through the cross of Jesus. You see, the Lord himself did the work for our salvation when he sent Jesus – the sinless One – to take our sin upon him and be executed for our sins. This is grace. Grace is God's doing! However, we *do* have a simple part to play in our salvation, but our part is simply to admit that we can't save ourselves! The only *effort* we put into our salvation is to admit that we are not saved by our *own effort* and to put confidence in God's effort through the cross. This is faith.

Grace and faith do apply to your salvation, but grace and faith apply also to the rest of your daily God-Tracking life. By grace God has given you his Word, and by faith you live by its precepts and promises. By grace God has given you the deposit of his Holy Spirit; by faith you live daily by the Spirit for a miraculous life. By grace God has empowered you to serve him and walk in holiness; by faith you grab hold of his purposes and live in his righteousness. Today, dear God-tracker, come to Jesus and make every effort to resign to God's grace.

⇨ READ ALL ABOUT IT!

John 3:1-21; Romans 5:2; Ephesians 2:8; 2 Corinthians 5:21; Romans 10:8-13; 2 Corinthians 12:9-10

Pray

"O Father, I understand now that I can do nothing to earn my salvation or to earn power for daily living. It's only by your grace – your effort – that I am made right before you and empowered to fulfil your purposes. So today I resign from my own effort to live a good life and I resign from my own effort to live a spiritual life. By faith I grab on to your forgiveness, your power and your glory. I repent of my sin and, by believing Jesus died and rose again, I confess him as Lord. Thank you that I am now born again. Lord, I now step out in faith and claim your power for purpose! In Jesus' name. Amen."

Week 17

GOD-TRACKING IS RESTING IN GOD'S PRESENCE

Isaiah 40:31

...but they who wait for the Lord shall renew their strength; they shall mount up with wings like eagles; they shall run and not be weary; they shall walk and not faint.

The scriptures tell us that a man plans his course in his heart but it's the Lord who determines his steps. This is because it is God who knows the plans he has for us; we don't. The concept of God-Tracking is seeking to stay on track with God's plans and God's purposes as he reveals them to us in his time.

The prophet Isaiah was a man who knew well what it meant to be a God-tracker. He was born to a privileged position in Jerusalem as cousin to King Uzziah. And yet Isaiah definitely did not rely on his royal heritage for purpose in life. On the contrary, during the reigns of three subsequent kings, he proved himself to be quite the thorn in the royal flesh. He believed that the Lord God had a clear plan for Jerusalem to maintain autonomy and mirror his glory at a time of greyed-out borders. One man against a whole parliament (or royal court) and yet he was strong, consistent and a sure God-tracker. So how did he do it?

Isaiah said, "He gives strength to the weary and increases the power of the weak." He went on to say that even youths grow tired and weary, but those whose hope is in the Lord would renew their strength. They would soar on wings like eagles; run and not grow weary; walk and not faint. In some Bible translations, the word "hope" is translated as "wait". Both words imply patiently resting in the power of God's *presence* as one waits for God's plans to be revealed. You see, it is only from within the presence of God that strength, hope and power for purpose will come to you. Waiting on the Lord in the hope of his promises, while standing strong in God's purposes, Isaiah went on to become one of the greatest prophets ever.

Whatever you're facing today, put your hope in God's plans and wait patiently for his every direction in life. As you wait, fill your heart and mind with the promises of God's Word. Hope in his purposes; remain in his presence and you will renew your strength. As Isaiah said, "In quietness and in trust shall be your strength." Therefore, rest in God's presence today and you'll find power for your purpose.

⇨ READ ALL ABOUT IT!

Proverbs 16:9; Jeremiah 29:11;

Isaiah 40:29-31; Isaiah 30:15

Pray

"Dear Lord, I am sorry for relying on my own strength and my own abilities as I face the difficulties of life. I admit I've been voicing my own opinion instead of quietly resting in your strength and your knowledge of my circumstances. I admit that I have been trying to work things out on my own instead of waiting for you to reveal your purposes to me. I'm weary, Lord. I confess you are God of my life and choose now to be still in your presence. I commit my paths to you and acknowledge you in all my ways. Your presence is my power for purpose. Amen."

Week 18

GOD-TRACKING IS ENDURING DESERT TRIALS BY THE STRENGTH OF GOD'S WORD

James 1:2-3

Consider it pure joy, my brothers, whenever you face trials of many kinds, because you know that the testing of your faith develops perseverance.

A young man approached John the Baptist to be baptised one morning. He was a confident young man and John knew him well. "I need to be baptized by you, and do you come to me?" said John. Jesus replied, "Let it be so now; it is proper for us to do this to fulfil all righteousness." John proceeded to baptise Jesus, and as Jesus came up out of the waters, the heavens opened. A voice said, "This is my Son, whom I love; with him I am well pleased." Immediately, Jesus was led by the Holy Spirit into the desert where Satan severely tested the Son of Man during a 40-day total fast.

Tracking the plans of God will sometimes lead you into desert places where your faith may be severely tested. You may be in such a place today. However, God's Word will always prepare you for difficult times ahead, as it did for Jesus. God is eternal and he knows your beginning from your end and because he loves you, he is already on the other side of your trial preparing your way. So, hold fast to the Father's promises and trust him to guide you through your desert trials.

I imagine Jesus took much courage in his Father's affirming words while he was being attacked by Satan in the desert. The Word of God prepared Jesus for all the trials that lay ahead … the desert and the cross!

⇨ **READ ALL ABOUT IT!**
Matthew 3:13-17; Matthew 4:1-11;
Proverbs 3:5-6; Hebrews 11:6

Pray

"Dear Abba Father, I am afraid of what lies ahead. The way I see things from here, there's not much hope for my success and happiness. I feel as though I am trudging through thick desert sands in the heat of the sun, weak and thirsty. And yet, I remember the words you spoke to Jesus before his desert trials, and I take courage.

In Christ, you call me son/daughter and you love me. Thank you for the strength this gives me. Thank you that my hope is not in my own way forward but in the way you have already prepared for me a place where you meet my needs and fulfil my dreams. My hope is in you and this hope will not disappoint me. Thank you, Lord. Amen."

Week 19

GOD-TRACKING IS ENDURING TRIALS IN CHRIST AS CHARACTER BUILDING

James 1:2

Consider it pure joy, my brothers, whenever you face trials of many kinds.

Let's face it, tracking God's plans can often become confusing when we experience difficulties in life. Surely, if I am acknowledging God in everything I do and sense his call on my life then all things will always work out easy for me. I shouldn't suffer difficulties like the next guy; after all, I'm a King's kid! Right?

Job was an average guy like you and me except his walk was blameless before God. You could say that Job was a God-tracker. He acknowledged the Lord in all he did and attempted to live a good life. In fact, the Bible describes Job as a man who feared God and shunned evil. However, one day it pleased God to give Job the trial of his life. We read in the book of Job that God allowed Satan to inflict Job with all manner of loss and difficulty, even though he was a good man. Job lost his children; he lost his wealth; and almost lost his life to a dreaded skin disorder. Nevertheless, we read that Job never "cursed God." In other words, he never questioned God's judgement or his sovereignty. In the end God speaks to Job and reminds him in no uncertain terms that he is God and Job is not! God reveals his sovereign right over the life and purposes of man and his right to produce endurance, faith and character through trials and difficulties for those whom he calls. Finally, at the end of the book of Job, we read these amazing words, "The Lord blessed the latter part of Job's life more than the first."

Job's experience helps us view our own trials in a new light. As God loved Job, so God loves you. Though Job suffered intense difficulty he continued to acknowledge God in all his ways. As a result, God restored Job to the extent that he was far better off after his trials than before. And God will restore you, too, if you continue to acknowledge God and keep your eyes on Jesus. The difference between Job and you, however, is Christ. In Job we discover a man standing before God by his own righteousness. As a Christian you stand before God by Christ's righteousness.

Unlike Job, your victory is not in your own goodness; rather it's in the righteousness of Jesus Christ. Apostle Paul says that through Christ you can face any difficulty, any loss and any trial. So, the next time you find yourself confused by trials and tribulations, just remember God is not testing *your righteousness*, he is *developing your character*.

⇨ READ ALL ABOUT IT!

The book of Job, especially note Job 42:12;

James 1:3-4

Pray

"Dear Lord, I'm sorry if I have flippantly joked about 'my crowns in glory' because of my trials on earth. There is nothing glib about the reward you have graciously reserved for me, both in glory and in this life. So, I joyfully face the tests you present me with. God, I thank you for your promises of blessing, provision and reward in my life. Thank you that you will get me through this time of difficulty. It feels as though my whole world is collapsing around my ears, but I know that you are in control. In faith I look forward to my rescue and thank you in advance for your healing, delivery and provision. You are God and I am not. Today I submit to your sovereignty in my life and choose to praise you in my time of trial. Thank you for my crown of life. Amen."

Week 20

GOD-TRACKING IS NEVER LOOKING DOWN IN THE TIME OF BATTLE!

Colossians 2:15

And having disarmed the powers and authorities, he made a public spectacle of them, triumphing over them by the cross.

Jehoshaphat dropped his head and gazed at the mosaic floor of his chamber. The messengers' words still rang in his ears, "A vast army is coming against you from Edom." This was a situation he'd feared for so long. He had dreaded an attack from the Moabites and Ammonites and now it was happening. Slowly raising his head, the king knew there was only one thing to do: enquire of Yahweh. Jehoshaphat called for a fast and prayed, "O Lord, God of our fathers, are you not the God who is in heaven? For we have no power to face this vast army that is attacking us. We do not know what to do, but our eyes are upon you." The reply of God came to him through the prophet, "Do not be afraid or discouraged because of this vast army. For the battle is not yours, but God's." While Jehoshaphat and the people of Judah were still praising God, the Lord set ambushes against their enemy and annihilated it. God was true to his word. The battle Jehoshaphat faced that day was the Lord's.

As God-trackers, we often face dreaded battles in life that appear to be beyond our control. But I believe the Lord is calling us to lift our gaze and fix our eyes on Jesus, who has already fought the fight and won the battle! When he died humbly at Calvary, he made a spectacle of the forces of evil. He has ridiculed sin, Satan and death itself. Today he is calling us to lift our heads and praise him in the face of our enemies.

Your fight is not against any man; it's against the forces of darkness. So, put on God's whole armour today, turn from sin and advance by faith. It only takes the smallest amount of faith to move a mountain. It's time for you to move forward and not backward; to look up and not down, forcefully advancing to take back your life from the devil. God knows the plans he has for you – good and great plans – so don't hold back. Like Jehoshaphat, lift your gaze and praise God in the face of your fight. After all, the battle is not yours but God's!

⇨ READ ALL ABOUT IT!

2 Chronicles 20:1-30; Hebrews 2:12; Colossians 2:15; Ephesians 6:10-17; 2 Corinthians 5:7; Matthew 17:20

Pray

"Dear God, I'm sorry for looking down in the face of battle. I consciously choose to look up, up into the eyes of Jesus! I repent of all sin I have committed in the past few days and choose to give no opportunity to Satan. As I face this battle I'm in, I will give you praise for the work of Jesus upon the cross. I confess that Jesus gained a spectacular victory at the cross over the devil and all his attempts at derailing me from your track for my life! Today I move forward and not backward; I look up, not down. Today I will not give up but will look up and forcefully regain this ground Satan has stolen in the name of Jesus, because I know the battle is not mine but yours! In Jesus' name. Amen."

Week 21

GOD-TRACKING IS KNOWING THAT GOD'S PLANS WILL ALWAYS WORK OUT FOR GOOD IN THE END

Romans 8:28

And we know that in all things God works for the good of those who love him, who have been called according to his purpose.

Paul and Barnabas had been traveling for some time together and had struck up a good relationship. Paul was the teacher and Barnabas was the encourager. Both had a part to play in the great scheme of God's purposes for the early Church to take the gospel to the ends of the earth.

Sometime after their first trip together when Paul suggested a second missionary trip, Barnabas wanted to take his cousin, John Mark, along with them. Mark had travelled with them on the first trip but, for some reason, he had deserted them halfway through, so Paul was reluctant to take him along on the second trip. This caused a rift between Paul and Barnabas. Barnabas then took John Mark on

81

an independent journey and continued to encourage this young man. Paul, on the other hand, decided to take a new young prodigy, Timothy, on his second missionary trip. "What a tragic affair," you might say. But was it?

Barnabas, the encourager, continued to encourage and prophesy God's Word wherever he travelled, with Mark close by his side. Mark was eventually to return to Jerusalem where he would sit at the feet of that great apostle and leader of the early Church, Simon Peter. Mark was an educated man; therefore, I like to think it was Barnabas who encouraged his cousin to sit under Peter's ministry and scribe the sermons and accounts of Peter's testimony of the story of Jesus. These writings were to later become part of Holy Bible known as the Gospel According to Mark.

Paul, the teacher, embarked upon his second missionary trip with Timothy by his side. They travelled far and wide preaching and teaching and planting churches. One church they planted was in Ephesus. Later, Timothy was to return to Ephesus and take up oversight of that great church. Paul then began writing his famous epistles, which included his pastoral epistles also now found in the Holy Bible. Two of these epistles include First and Second Timothy.

So, it is we see what appeared to be a tragic rift between two great men (who were later powerfully reconciled, by the way) had led to the development of two more great men of God. And this apparent disagreement over travel plans between Paul and Barnabas had likewise resulted in the writing of three powerful books that have been preserved for centuries in the Holy Bible; books that still change lives today. On the outside, it seemed God's plan was being thwarted by Paul and Barnabas' disagreement, but on the inside, God was at work! The One who knows the beginning from the end was carefully strategizing the lives of these men for his own supreme and eternal purposes, turning a bad situation into something very good. Perhaps God is doing the same in your life today.

⇨ READ ALL ABOUT IT!
Acts 15; Gospel of Mark; 1 and 2 Timothy;
Romans 8:26-30

Pray

"Lord, so often it seems as though my life is falling apart. Sometimes it feels people are ganging up against me and opposing my every move. Other times it seems as though circumstances just don't seem to work out the way I'd hoped. But I see today that you can take any situation in my life – good or bad – and turn it out for the good, always! Dear Lord, I submit myself to your plans and to your purposes. Help me not to become despondent by apparent conflicting circumstances in my life. So do whatever it takes to lead

my life according to your will. Help me to trust you when things seem to go wrong, as I continue to acknowledge you in all my ways. Praise you Lord. Amen."

Week 22

GOD-TRACKING IS FOLLOWING GOD'S NAVIGATION ALL THE WAY

2 Corinthians 5:7

... for we walk by faith, not by sight.

One of the most ridiculous satellite navigation stories I ever heard involved a 67-year-old Belgian lady who set out on a 34-mile journey to fetch a friend from her local airport. She programmed her GPS device for directions to the airport but somehow entered the wrong information. When she neared the exit to the airport the device instructed her to continue going. Obediently she followed the electronic voice and kept on going and going and going without stopping, except for fuel. Finally, two days later, after crossing five international borders and ignoring French and German signs she arrived at Zagreb station, Croatia! When asked why she had not noticed that she was so far from home she simply replied, "I didn't ask myself any questions. I was just distracted, so I kept my foot down."

God-Tracking is a bit like navigating by satellite navigation. When we give our lives to Jesus, we consciously surrender our lives to navigate by his voice every step of the way. However, the difference between navigating our God-tracks by Christs' directions and navigating the highways with a GPS is, Christ cannot be programmed by us! When we acknowledge the Lord in all our ways we surrender the right to selfishly programme our own lives and choose to submit to his directions along life's highways and byways.

In that new job or house move you are facing today, tune into your Lord's voice and follow his roadmap. In that relationship issue you're dealing with or that new business venture you're planning, be sure to acknowledge God in prayer and allow him to programme your life's journey. Keep your foot down and keep driving; turn only when he says turn and stop only when he says "Stop!" And whatever you do don't become distracted by the world's commentary on your life's journey or you will soon find yourself programmed to become lost.

⇨ READ ALL ABOUT IT!
Proverbs 3:5-6; Ephesians 3:20-21; Psalm 119:105

Pray

"O Lord my God, I'm sorry for trying to programme my own life's track. I'm sorry, too, for tuning into the world's commentary on life and allowing it to influence my thinking. I know that only Jesus is the life, the truth... and the way! So, Lord, be my way in this life! Help me in all the situations that I face to keep my eyes on Jesus and my ears open to so that I will make the right decisions, as I acknowledge you in all my ways. I seek your hand; I seek your voice; and I seek your face. Help me to live by your directions and not by my human reason. In Jesus' name I pray. Amen."

.

Week 23

GOD-TRACKING IS STANDING SURE IN IN THE "YES AND AMEN" OF GOD'S PROMISES FOR YOUR FUTURE

Philippians 1:6

...being confident of this, that he who began a good work in you will carry it on to completion until the day of Christ Jesus.

God's Word, the Bible, is packed with God's promises for those who love and serve him through Jesus Christ. For instance, God has promised eternal life, forgiveness of sin, healing for the sick, provision for the needy, joy for the grieving and peace for the anxious. I also believe that the Lord has a unique promise for you to fulfil the plans he has for your life. His plans are always good and his plans never come undone. And here's the proverbial cherry on the top of the cream cake: *all of God's promises are "yes" and "amen" through the Lord Jesus Christ!*

As you read these words here today and look up the scriptures listed below, I believe the Lord will give you a specific word for your future. I believe God's plans for you are definitely not over, no matter your age or social circumstances. In fact, I believe God's purposes for those who seek to track his will are never over until the day they breathe their last breath on earth and go home to their Lord in glory. As you read these words here today, I believe that God's word to you is still: *I know the plans I have for you, plans for well-being and not for evil, to give you a future and a hope.*

You may have recently been praying about a new opportunity or waiting for the Lord to prompt a decision that you are about to make, a decision that will perhaps change your life. God may have plans for you in a new venture that will end up bending you or manipulating you in ways you may never expect but know this, he will never leave you to face changes alone. His word is always true and his way is perfect; the word of the Lord is flawless and he is a shield for all who take refuge in him.

If you're feeling challenged by changes or new prospects today; if you feel the adventure of your life intensifying then perhaps the Holy Spirit is saying to you, "I love it when a plan comes together!" So, stand sure in his promises to you today and shout out a resounding *amen*, in Christ!

⇨ **READ ALL ABOUT IT!**

Jeremiah 29:11; John 3:16; 1 John 1:9; 1 Peter 2:24;

Philippians 4:19; Isaiah 61:3; Philippians 4:6;

2 Corinthians 1:20; Psalm 18:30

Pray:

"Dear Lord, your word instructs me to not treat prophecy with contempt but to test everything and only hold onto that which is good. So, this word that I have read here today I test in Jesus' name. Help me to only follow that which you have purposed for my life. And so, dear Lord, I ask for your blessing upon every decision I make today. I look for your hand and your guidance for my future as I continue to acknowledge you in all my ways. Today I commit myself to serve you and make the most of every opportunity you bring my way, with wisdom from your Spirit. Help me to have the faith to step out and grab hold of every promise you have for me. And I pray for strength to endure the bending and re-shaping that I may need to endure to follow your new plans in my life. Jesus, I am yours! Amen."

Week 24

GOD-TRACKING IS WATCHING FOR GOD TO ACTIVATE HIS PROMISES TO YOU

James 1:17

Every good and perfect gift is from above, coming down from the Father of the heavenly lights, who does not change like shifting shadows.

Lucy looked at me suspiciously, "Do you really mean to say that God loves me no matter what I've done in my life?"

"Yes," I said with a grin. I could see that God's Word was penetrating her hard-core 21st-century young mind-set. "Why don't you join our Bible studies? You'll be able to ask any question you like, and I'm sure God will help you understand more about what Jesus has done for you on the cross."

Lucy began attending the Bible studies, but after a short while she stopped. I didn't see her again until many years later when she walked into our church unannounced. I was very surprised to see her. I'd given up on Lucy, assuming she had strayed from God's truth. But there she was, hands raised and worshiping the Lord. As soon as

I had closed the meeting, I made my way to her. "Wow, I never thought I'd see you in church, Lucy. How are you?" Lucy excitedly explained how she had moved away but could never forget the words she heard at those Bible studies. "So, have you given your life to Christ?" I pressed hesitantly. I received a resounding, "Yes!"

God once called a young man named Jeremiah to be his prophet to rebellious Israel. Jeremiah was timid and fearful so God promised to fill the young prophet's mouth with his Word. Then God gave Jeremiah a vision of an almond branch and asked him what he saw. Jeremiah replied that he saw a branch of an almond tree. Then the Lord said, "You have seen correctly, for I am watching to see that my Word is fulfilled." Almonds are very prolific in Israel, but God was doing more than giving young Jeremiah a lesson in horticulture. The word for almond in Hebrew is pronounced, *shaw-kade*, while the Hebrew word for watching is pronounced, *shaw-kad*. God was using a pun in Jeremiah's language to help him understand that when God speaks, he watches over his Words to activate his promises in his time. That is, when God makes a promise, he keeps it!

By God's grace, I had spoken his Word to young Lucy and had almost forgotten about her after she'd moved away. But God's Word – the seed of her salvation – had been planted in her heart. It was not up to me to convince her to become a Christian. God, by his Holy Spirit, was quite capable for doing that. He had promised to watch over the Word I'd spoken into Lucy's life. For several years, the Lord watered that seed and nurtured it until Lucy was ready to receive them. Under the inspiration of the Holy Spirit, she responded and asked Christ into her life.

Dear God-tracker, it could be that God has made a promise to you. Perhaps he has given you a promise about a loved one for whom you have been praying many years to become a Christian. Or perhaps he has called you into service and promised to meet all your needs as you step out in faith. Whatever it is the Lord God has promised you, by his Word he will fulfil his promise, in his time. So, why not put an almond in your pocket to remind you that God watches over his Word?

⇨ READ ALL ABOUT IT!
Jeremiah 1:11-12; Isaiah 55:8-13; Matthew 6:25-34;
2 Corinthians 1:18-20

Pray

"Thank you, my Lord, that you love me so much that you remain faithful to your promises to me. Even though it seems as though I don't see any results of my prayers yet, I know you are watching over your Word in my life and will bring about those answers in your time. Thank you for promising to meet all my needs and heal my body.

Thank you for promising to bring my loved ones to Christ. Thank you, too, for the hope I have that you will guide me in every aspect of my life. I commit my ways to you and stand on the promises of your Word today. Praise you, my God. Amen."

Week 25

GOD-TRACKING IS LOOKING BACK TO SEE AN OPEN DOOR

2 Corinthians 9:8

And God is able to make all grace abound to you, so that in all things at all times, having all that you need, you will abound in every good work.

Diana Ross popularized the theme to the film *Mahogany*, which posed the question, "Do you know where you're going to?" This song is packed with questions about life and goes on to ask, "Do you get what you're hoping for? When you look behind you there's no open door. What are you hoping for?" I think this song demonstrates a life filled with "pipedreams," "if onlies" and "what ifs." Sadly, many of us find ourselves caught up in the same guessing game, not sure where we are going to.

But as God-trackers we should exercise a completely different approach to life because we believe in the purposes of God. Indeed, without Christ I'd have no idea where I was going to, but because I confess Jesus as my Lord and God, I can be confident that he will direct my path. God-Tracking is based on the precept that God knows the plans he has for us (and only God knows these plans) and if we acknowledge him in all our ways, then he will guide us according to these plans he has for us. Therefore, in faith I can commit my future to him in the hope that the doors he opens for me will work out for my good and his glory. And faith is being confident in things hoped for.

So, whatever it is you are hoping for, you can be confident He knows where you are going to. Even though you can't see what tomorrow holds, the doors God opens no man can close! Therefore, if you walk by faith and not by sight, when you look behind you, you will see an open door.

⇨ READ ALL ABOUT IT!
Proverbs 3:5-6; Jeremiah 29:11; Romans 8:28-31; Hebrews 11:1; Revelation 3:7-8

Pray
"My Lord, thank you for the plans that you have for my life. Thank you for the many doors you have waiting to be opened to me. Today I re-confess that I acknowledge your Lordship and purposes in every aspect of my life – my career, my relationships, my church life, my private life – and trust that you will open those doors for me that

comply with your plans. Help me to walk in faith even when I can't see what awaits me on the other side of the door and to live in expectation that I will receive what I am hoping for. Lord, I love you and I trust that all things will work out for my good and your glory. Amen."

Week 26

GOD-TRACKING IS NEVER LOOKING FOR SHORTCUTS

Psalm 25:4

Show me your ways, O LORD, teach me your paths.

From my bedroom window I could see the police car parked out of sight, waiting in ambush for the unsuspecting motorist to skip the stop sign. A short one-way street served as an access to our suburb from the main carriageway a block away. It was the only way into our neighbourhood at that point. If a driver took this access unintentionally, he'd need to make a long winding detour to return to the carriageway. As I watched, a car came down the one-way and, not stopping at the stop sign, made an illegal U-turn and fled the wrong way back up the one-way. "You're nicked!" I said out loud as the cop car's blue lights flashed and sirens wailed.

In my walk with God, I have discovered that if I acknowledge God in all my ways, he will always direct me on his paths for my life. This implies prayerfully seeking and confessing God in every decision I make – every turn, every stop and every U-turn. I have discovered that, if I do this, I will inevitably wind up on the right road. However, there are the times when, although I have acknowledged God in this way, I find myself making a hasty wrong decision and end up turning off his pathway at that point in my life. However, because I *have* acknowledged God, he graciously leads me back to where he intended me to be, albeit the long way around. You see, dear God-tracker, if you go off-track there are no shortcuts back to God's path.

If you find today that you have made choices outside of God's will; or if you have not acknowledged God in a decision and find that you're off his track for your life; don't take another step without committing your ways to God. It could also be that you have acknowledged God in a recent decision but have attempted to take a short cut to gain access to his purpose. If that's you, then don't try and force your way back to where you left the road. Rather seek God's word and allow it to illuminate your pathway once again. Then follow God's "diversion" signs until you come back to where you left your life's track. You may even be astounded at the scenic view along the way.

⇨ **READ ALL ABOUT IT!**
Proverbs 3:5-6; Luke 13:22-30;
Psalm 119:105-110; Psalm 25:1-5

Pray

"Dear Lord I have always tried to acknowledge you in all my decisions, but sometimes find myself going off-track because of wrong choices. Please forgive me for any selfish decision I've made or for attempting to take a short cut to your will. I confess now that you are my Lord and I re-acknowledge you in every aspect of my life. Open your Word to me and guide me by your Holy Spirit to find my way back to the road you have planned for me. I believe, because I have acknowledged you in all I do, you will help me find my way back to your plan for my life. Amen."

Week 27

GOD-TRACKING IS FLOURISHING AT EVERYTHING YOU DO, IN CHRIST

Proverbs 10:22

The blessing of the LORD brings wealth, and he adds no trouble to it.

I know a Christian man who believed he had what it took to make it big in business, so he left a secure job to open a private health centre. He took out a loan and rented premises. Equipping it with all the mod cons of gym tech he opened the doors to the public. However, his business venture failed. After some months of loss and growing debts, he closed the gym and attempted to find a new job. Sadly, he was unsuccessful and eventually his bank foreclosed on his house. He lost everything. He and his little family moved in with his wife's parents, destitute and disappointed.

During this time of heart-searching, my friend realised in his striving to make a quick buck, he had slipped off his God-track. He'd taken his eyes off Christ and away from his Word and thought he could do it alone. Now humbled, he repented and reaffirmed his walk with God. However, my friend still had the desire to flourish, but now realised he would never succeed in business doing things *his way*. He realised to truly succeed in life; he would need God's blessing on all his efforts. My friend knew that this would require acknowledging God in his business plans and seeking to honour him with every penny he earned. After some time and with a little help, he was able to start a new business. Now, with a new heart, he acknowledged God in prayer, in business ethics and in giving. Soon his new business became very successful and he began to flourish in every aspect of his life to the extent that he became a source of provision to many other people in need.

You too can flourish in every avenue of your life if you continually acknowledge God in all your ways and seek first his kingdom principles. Unlike my friend's first attempt to do things his way, if you make God your partner, you will be successful in every walk of life. Jesus flourished in his ministry as healer, teacher and Saviour with the words of the Eternal Father ringing in his ears, "This is my Son whom I love, and with him I am well pleased." Even in his work in dying for our sins, Jesus flourished by rising from the dead. In Christ you are forgiven and made righteous. Therefore, don't walk in the counsel of the wicked or stand in the way of sinners but delight yourself in the Lord and all you do will prosper.

 **READ ALL ABOUT IT!**

Proverbs 3:5-6; Proverbs 16:3; Matthew 3:16-17

Matthew 6:33; Romans 8:35-39; Psalm 1

Pray

"Dear God, I am sorry for going it alone. I realise that I cannot be truly successful at anything I do without your blessing. Therefore, today I reaffirm my acknowledgement of you as Lord of my relationships, my business, my career and my recreational life. I take my eyes off of self and fix them on Jesus, author of my faith. I commit my plans to you and seek your hand on all I set my hand to do. Lord, guide me in my choices and help me to be successful, according to your will for my life. In you I know I can flourish! Amen."

Week 28

GOD-TRACKING IS COLLECTING HIS TROPHIES OF GRACE

1 Corinthians 9:24

Do you not know that in a race all the runners run, but only one gets the prize? Run in such a way as to get the prize.

The priests were still standing with the Ark of the Covenant on their shoulders in the middle of the muddied riverbed. A few hours earlier Joshua instructed them to step out boldly into the flooding Jordan River saying that God would stop its flow so the Israelites could cross over into the Promised Land. Obediently they'd done so and witnessed a great miracle as the waters of the flowing Jordan piled up upstream, causing a clear pathway through the river where they stood. Now, as they waited their next instruction, they watched as twelve men came back to the middle of the riverbed, collecting twelve rocks from where they stood. These men proceeded to pile these rocks up on the west bank of the Jordan as a monument to God's provision – twelve trophies to remember how God had delivered his people from slavery, brought them through a desert wilderness for 40 years and across a flooding river on dry ground to possess the land he'd promised their forefathers. Twelve trophies of God's grace!

What is a trophy? To me a trophy is an award for a race well run. A trophy can be a medal, a cup or a crown. When we receive a trophy, we put it up somewhere in a place where it will be noticed as a reminder of our achievement. A trophy reminds us of our persistence, excellence and success. Whenever we gaze at it, it motivates us to run the next race in such a way as to win the prize, again!

God has a purpose for your life. Perhaps he has made you a promise that he will take you on to his "Promised Land" for you, but you may still need to cross a flooding river to arrive there. As you face this challenge, gaze again upon the trophies he has awarded you in life and remember the great things you have already done through him. Allow God's trophies to motivate you to run that next race well. Then make your way across your next river collecting more memories of his provision, blessing and guidance along the way and then carry them on into battle on the other side as trophies of God's grace.

⇨ **READ ALL ABOUT IT!**

1 Corinthians 9:24-27; Hebrews 12:1-3; Psalm 44:1-8

Pray

"Dear God, thank you for all the times you have come through for me and for all the wonderful memories I have collected along the way. Thank you for my trophies of your grace. I want to erect a monument to your honour in my life, made up of all these blessings, provisions, miracles and answers to prayers you have brought about. I want to gaze upon them time and again and praise your name for your goodness to me. These trophies always serve to motivate me to run this race with perseverance, knowing that what you have done before, you can do again. Help me now to face this new river with confidence and cross over to enjoy the promises you have given me. I know there may still be difficulties on the other side of the river, but I will carry your trophies of grace into battle to remind me of my victory in Jesus. Amen."

Week 29

GOD-TRACKING IS FOLLOWING YOUR DREAMS BY GOD'S GRACE, IN SPITE OF DISAPPOINTMENT

2 Thessalonians 2:16-17

May our Lord Jesus Christ himself and God our Father,
who loved us and by his grace gave us eternal
encouragement and good hope, encourage your hearts
and strengthen you in every good deed and word.

Colin grew up in a very sheltered home environment. He attended Sunday School every Sunday where he heard many wonderful stories about God. He loved these stories and firmly believed in the God of the Bible. At the tender age of 10, young Colin gave his heart to Jesus, was baptised by the age of 14 and baptised in the Holy Spirit by 16. Like any boy of his age, Colin had dreams of grandeur, but sadly he was never given the opportunity to explore his dreams. He grew up in a very controlled and restricted environment. He had very few friends and was seldom allowed out the home. Now, looking back on his early life, Colin realised he was consumed with anger

113

and bitterness for a childhood wasted. "How could God have allowed me to grow up so stifled?" he would often think.

Disappointment can lead to despair, despair can lead to anger, and anger to bitterness. Bitterness consumes the soul and manifests as unforgiveness and vengeance. Grace, on the other hand, liberates the soul and gains victory! Jesus took all the consequences of sin upon himself when he went to the cross. Those consequences included disappointment, despair, anger, bitterness and unforgiveness. Didn't he pray, "Father forgive them for they do not know what they are doing?" Jesus was abused and beaten then mercilessly executed on trumped-up charges, yet he was not consumed with bitterness, even after his resurrection. The Bible tells us to look to Jesus and follow his example of how he looked through the trial of the cross and saw himself victorious on the other side.

If Colin had learned earlier in life to look beyond his circumstances and see himself as God saw him then he would have grown into the man of influence and wonder he dreamed of becoming. In the process of seeking to track God's plans for his life, if Colin had acknowledged that his Lord and God was already on the other side of his trials, then he would not have been so consumed with bitterness. And if Colin had walked in forgiveness grown from grace, he would have realised that God's grace was sufficient to guide him toward those dreams of grandeur.

⇨ **READ ALL ABOUT IT!**
Luke 23:32-35; Hebrews 12:2-3; 2 Corinthians 12:7-10

Pray

"Dear Lord, I want to ask your forgiveness for holding so many grudges in my life. Lord, I'm sorry for any bitterness and unforgiveness that I harbour. Father forgive my sins as I forgive those who have sinned against me. I choose now to let go of all grievances I hold against people who have offended me. I let it all go and choose to show grace to those who have hurt me. Thank you for your grace to me in dealing with my past and looking to the future. Lord, it's only by your grace that I am what I am and by your grace that I will be what you plan for me to be. Your grace is enough. Amen."

If you want us to pray with you then e-mail
dudley@surereality.net

Or scan the Q.R. code below.

Week 30

GOD-TRACKING IS BELIEVING THAT YOU ARE GOD'S HANDIWORK

Psalm 139:16-17

...your eyes saw my unformed body. All the days ordained for me were written in your book before one of them came to be. How precious to me are your thoughts, O God! How vast is the sum of them!

I'm told that our chromosomes contain all the genetic information that makes us human and unique individuals. The Human Genome project was a project set up to discover how many genes make up each of the 46 human chromosomes that each of us have. In this research it was discovered that the human genome contains approximately 3 billion base pairs of genes. The human genome is the map of genetic information that makes you a human being and not a monkey. And yet, I'm told, the genetic difference between humans and chimpanzees is only 4% at most. This implies that each of us is up to 96% similar to a chimpanzee. And yet, have you ever heard of a chimp that may have painted the Sistine Chapel ceiling,

117

or written a play like *Othello*? Likewise, have you ever heard of a chimpanzee which has walked on the moon or deciphered his own genome?

The Bible tells us that God is the creator of all that exists. He created everything from a subatomic electron to a supernova, from a bacterium to a blue whale. And God created you and me, just as we are. Listen: "For you created my inmost being; you knit me together in my mother's womb. I praise you because I am fearfully and wonderfully made; your works are wonderful; I know that full well." It is also written that, in Christ, we are a peculiar people. Peculiar? Yes, indeed; if you know Christ, then you are peculiar to him!

You are God's handiwork. He formed you in your mother's womb with 46 chromosomes containing approximately 3 billion base pairs of genes in every nucleus of every cell in your body. You are his workmanship, created in Christ Jesus for good works, which God prepared beforehand, that you should walk in them. Some people think they are of no value, but every person is unique and of supreme value to his Creator. The omniscient Lord God Almighty, who knit you together as an embryo, has foreknowledge of every moment of your life. He even loved you so much that, while you were still a sinner, Christ died for you. God does all things on purpose, so step out in faith and lay hold of that opportunity. No matter what anybody says, you are worth it!

 **READ ALL ABOUT IT!**

Genesis 1 & 2; Psalm 139; 1 Peter 2:9-10;

Romans 5:6-11; Ephesians 3:10

Pray

"O Lord my Father, I realise now that I am valued. Thank you that you love me so much that you not only saved me from sin and death but have designed the course of my life. I believe this course is to bless me and prosper me. You say in the Bible that you know the plans you have for my future. Today I want to submit to your design and seek your perfect plan for my life. Help me to make the most of every opportunity, with wisdom. Dear Lord, thank you for those around me who love me. Help me to change my own attitude regarding my life so I may walk in the confidence that I am your handiwork. Amen."

Week 31

GOD-TRACKING RESULTS IN GOOD
PRODUCE FROM PRUNED BRANCHES

John 15:16

You did not choose me, but I chose you and appointed you to go and bear fruit–fruit that will last. Then the Father will give you whatever you ask in my name.

On more than one occasion Jesus used a vineyard or workers of a vineyard as the subjects of his parables. Growing up in Israel, he would have understood well the finer principles associated with nurturing the vine to produce the best and most succulent grapes. Jesus knew how important it was to annually cut back a vine so that it will both grow well and produce better fruit.

Jesus said, "I am the true vine, and my Father is the gardener. He cuts off every branch in me that bears no fruit, while every branch that does bear fruit he prunes so that it will be even more fruitful." Then later he said, "I am the vine; you are the branches." By this analogy Jesus is referring to vineyard husbandry, which includes pruning back the plants each year so that their growing energies will go into producing better fruit. Just as a vineyard keeper would prune the vines in this way, so the Father cuts away the dead wood or malformed branches from the true Vine so it will produce a better crop.

You may feel as though you're being pruned right now. There may be circumstances or situations in your life that have died off or become malformed through the course of time. These could include a bad habit, a wrong relationship or a wrong involvement. God could be pruning your vine today, removing apathy, indifference or pessimism. Whatever it is that you feel is being cut off, you can be sure that you will not be left naked or abandoned in any way. Jesus said that God cuts off the branches that bear no fruit so those that do, will produce even more fruit. Be encouraged, dear God-tracker, God is removing from you those things that are timewasters or soul-destroyers. The Lord will never cut back anything that is to your benefit. And believe me when I tell you, unless God cuts out the dead wood from your life, you will never be fully productive. God desires for you to produce *good results* in your studies, your career, your home life and your church life. Your Father is pruning you so that you will produce *good fruit* in your relationships, your work and your commitments. So, embrace the pruning of the vineyard Keeper so that your harvest may be plentiful!

⇨ READ ALL ABOUT IT!

John 15; Galatians 5:16-25

Pray

"Dear Father, I know there are many areas of my life that need to be pruned back. I submit them to you today. I repent of those things that are grievous to your Spirit and seek to live a productive life according to your purposes for me. Lord, I open myself to your pruning. I ask that as you cut away the dead and malformed branches so that I will produce better product in my life. Bless my output. Bless all my efforts to serve you and cause me to produce good fruit for your kingdom; fruit that will be a blessing to those around me and, ultimately, a blessing to me, too. In Jesus' name. Amen."

Week 32

GOD-TRACKING IS HOLDING A SHORT ACCOUNT OF SIN!

Romans 6:11

In the same way, count yourselves dead to sin but alive to God in Christ Jesus.

A story is told of an eagle that was perched on a block of ice floating down the river above Niagara Falls. The swift current carried the ice and its regal passenger closer to the edge of the great precipice. Other birds and animals cried out, warning the eagle of the imminent danger that lay ahead but he thought he knew better. "I have great and powerful wings," he boasted. "I can fly from my perch at any time. I can handle it." Suddenly the edge of the falls was upon him. The torrent of water rushed the block of ice over the great falls. The mighty eagle spread his powerful wings to rise over the impending doom only to discover, too late, that his claws had become frozen fast to the cake of ice that he was standing on.

Dear God-tracker, as Christians you and I are not exempt from temptation, and sadly we often succumb to it and sin. I would that I didn't sin but, if I'm honest, I do. Even though I am born-again and a new creation in Jesus, I often still find the lure of the world tempting at times. Sadly, I often find myself doing things I wish I had not done and not doing things I wish I had done. Paul the Apostle had this dilemma, too. He once said, "I do not understand what I do. For what I want to do I do not do, but what I hate I do." And he said, "For the sinful nature desires what is contrary to the Spirit, and the Spirit what is contrary to the sinful nature. They conflict with each other, so that you do not do what you want."

Sin's like that. It's a block of ice. Stand long on it and you will become frozen by its icy grip. Sin entered the world when man disobeyed God's eternal Word and has held us fast since Eden. The Bible says that if we claim to be without sin, we deceive ourselves and the truth is not in us. But it also says that if we confess our sins, he is faithful and just and will forgive us our sins and purify us from all unrighteousness. What hope!

If you have come to Christ and consider yourself born-again then you *are* a new creation, indeed, and God *has* removed *all* your sin from you – both universal sin and committed sin. This occurred at your confession of Christ as Lord when God wiped your slate clean. However, from time to time you and I drop our guard and land back on that block of ice in the river. There, if we linger too long, sin will freeze around our ankles and hold us fast. So, when you find your feet getting cold don't waste a single minute. Admit your sin to the Lord and repent of it so that when you approach the waterfall you can soar on wings like an eagle.

⇨ READ ALL ABOUT IT!
Romans 7:14-20; Galatians 5:16-18; 1 John 1:8-10; Isaiah 40:28-31

Pray

"Dear God, I want to keep a short account of my sins. I realise that, even as a God- tracker, I do still sin from time to time and I am sorry, Lord. Therefore, I admit to you that I have recently done, said and thought things that I know grieve your Spirit and I'm sorry. O Father, your grace is the blowtorch that melts the ice of sin from around my ankles. Thank you for your grace. It is only by your grace that I can face another day in this world riddled with sin. Thank you for your mercy and forgiveness. Reveal to me when I am sinning, my God, and help me to repent daily so that I may draw closer to you as I track the paths of life. In the name of Jesus Christ, I pray. Amen."

Week 33

GOD-TRACKING IS COMING HUMBLY HUNGRY TO HIS TABLE

Psalm 23:5

You prepare a table before me in the presence of my enemies; you anoint my head with oil; my cup overflows.

When I came home from the office on Tuesday afternoon, I was not a little hungry. As I walked through the front door, I was hit by the aroma of a delicious spicy curry coming from the kitchen. My empty tummy performed cartwheels! "How far is dinner?" I asked my lovely wife as she stirred a steaming pot on the cooker. "Probably another half hour," she replied.

I knew I'd never make it. When I'm hungry, I am blinded to all good reason so I invaded the snack box. *Hmm… a chocolate bar, perhaps.* I munched a snack before supper. Thirty minutes later when I finally sat down with the family to consume that scrumptious curry my wife had so lovingly prepared, I was disappointed to discover that I was no longer hungry.

The Lord our God is magnificent, almighty and all-powerful. In fact, God is so great and infinite that we would never be able – in this life – to know any real measure of his fullness. Nevertheless, we are called to seek him with all our hearts and be filled with the Spirit. We're encouraged to be hungry for his righteousness. And, like blind Bartimaeus, we need to cry out to be touched by Jesus without giving up. Indeed, we need to come to him just as we are – empty and humbly hungry.

I encourage you today to not snack before dinner. Don't allow yourself to be filled up what the world offers, before coming to Jesus. Humbly come to him with an empty spiritual tummy; hungry for what only he can give you. The Psalms tell us that he prepares a table for us before our enemies. So come hungry to the banquet he has fixed for you, hungry for that Deposit from heaven. Only he can truly satisfy your cravings and your longings. Only he can truly fulfil your purposes and ambitions. His presence is all you need today, tomorrow and for the rest of your life.

⇨ READ ALL ABOUT IT!

Hebrew 11:6; Ephesians 5:18; Mark 10:46-52; Matthew 5:6; Matthew 11:28-29; Psalm 23:3-6

Pray

"Father God, thank you for sending Jesus to pay for my sins and thank you for sending the Holy Spirit to be my comforter and my companion. I confess Jesus as my Lord and humbly seek a greater touch from your Spirit. Lord, I open my heart to you and lay down all my preconceived notions and opinions. Forgive me for snaking on what this world offers. I want to be hungry for you and only you. Show me your glory. I come just as I am, humbly hungry to gain a greater touch of your holy goodness in my life. Amen."

Week 34

GOD-TRACKING IS SINKING YOUR ROOTS DEEP INTO GOD'S WORD IN SEARCH OF HIS LIVING WATER

John 6:35

Then Jesus declared, "I am the bread of life. He who comes to me will never go hungry, and he who believes in me will never be thirsty."

The tender sapling was just 1-year-old yet he knew well the taste of drought. As an acorn, he had not fallen far from the mighty Oak as it grew near the river. His young roots had quickly sprouted and found living water. The little acorn soon germinated into a strapping young plant. But now, somehow, the river's water seemed out of reach. There was only one thing the small tree could do: extend his roots down deeper into the substrate of the earth in search of that life-giving moisture.

Like all plants, a tree is comprised primarily of two main sections: one above ground and the other beneath the surface. The leaves, branches and trunk – the section above ground – are only as secure and healthy as its root system beneath the earth. The roots absorb both nutrients from the soil and water from between the particles of earth. Without water the plant will die. Therefore, when dry seasons come along, a tree will focus its energies on root development, digging deeper into the substrate of the earth in search of that life-giving moisture.

The Bible tells us the righteous man who walks honourably before God is like a tree planted by streams of water, delighting in God's word. As Christians, we have been made righteous before God through the death and resurrection of Jesus Christ. This means that, by grace, your sins have been atoned for and, by faith, you have been credited with God's righteousness. Therefore, you are that righteous man or woman who walks honourably before God. As such you have been planted by streams of living water.

However, from time to time it often seems as though we're living in a drought, even though we're still firmly planted by the river. Your enemy, the devil, is continually seeking to drag you away from God's perfect will for your life and will do all in his power to dry up the stream of God's blessings for you. So, if you feel as though your stream has dried up, sink your roots down deeper into the substrate of God's word and draw that living water from his Holy Spirit. And here's the promise: you will yield your fruit in season your leaf will not wither and whatever you do will prosper!

 **READ ALL ABOUT IT!**
Psalm 1; 1 Corinthians 5:21;
John 4:7-15; Matthew 4:4

Pray

"Lord, it feels as though I'm going through a drought again. Like that sapling, I know I was originally planted alongside a mighty river but somehow it seems as though that river has dried up. So today I make a conscious decision to sink my roots down deeper into your Word that I may find the life-giving moisture of your presence once again. I will not take note of Satan's attempt to dry up the flow of your blessings. Instead, I will reach out deeper by faith into your promises. Lord, I claim your blessings and your healing. Lord, I claim your fullness and your anointing on everything in my life as I continue to acknowledge you in all I do. Thank you for your living water. Amen."

Week 35

GOD-TRACKING IS MEASURING YOUR FAITH BY THE MEASURE OF HIS WORD

2 Corinthians 5:7
We live by faith, not by sight.

Did you know that it takes faith to breathe? How can I be sure there will still be sufficient oxygen with every breath I take? By some freak of nature, all the oxygen in the atmosphere might vanish before my next breath. Yikes! By the Holy Spirit, Paul writes in Romans 12 that we should have a sober judgement of ourselves according to the *measure of faith that God has given us.* You see, each person on earth has been given a degree of faith. It's by this measure of faith that I take every new breath in the confidence that there will be sufficient oxygen in the air in my lungs to keep me alive.

Paul begins this discussion by reminding us to modify our thinking; to be transformed from the pattern of the world by the renewal of our minds. Sadly, although we take certain measures of faith for granted (like breathing), when it comes to having confidence in the guidance of an inaudible and invisible God of love, we flounder around like headless chickens. Scripture tells that faith pleases God; therefore, we are to live by faith and not by sight. And living by faith requires a change in thinking.

Unfortunately, the world has formatted our minds to expect the worst of any situation or doubt we can make sensible life decisions, because we can't see into the future. Indeed, I can't see into tomorrow – but God can! I know that he is already there making provision for me and opening and closing doors according to his plans and purposes for my life. However, I can't see the future. All I can see is today. This is why I need to renew the way I look at my tomorrow by filling my mind with the promises and directions of God's Word. Faith comes from hearing the Word of God!

If you're facing a daunting decision today or seeking guidance for future choices, you'll need to renew your thinking about tomorrow. God's Word will not only increase the measure of faith, but it will guide your paths according to his will. So, ask the Lord God Almighty to help you make those decisions today for tomorrow. Then simply go ahead and make that decision in the knowledge of his Word, using your measure of faith!

 **READ ALL ABOUT IT!**

Romans 12:1-8; Hebrew 11:6; Romans 10:17

Pray

"Dear Father, I want to thank you for giving me a measure of faith. Thank you that I can live and breathe in the knowledge that you hold my tomorrow in your hands. Thank you that your Word increases my faith. Help me to read it more and to hear your directions for my future. In faith today I pledge myself to make the decisions I'm faced with according to your perfect will for my life. Let everything work out well in accordance with your purposes and provision. In the name of the Lord Jesus Christ, I pray. Amen."

Week 36

GOD-TRACKING IS BELIEVING THAT NOTHING CAN SEPARATE YOU FROM HIS LOVE

Romans 8:35

Who shall separate us from the love of Christ? Shall trouble or hardship or persecution or famine or nakedness or danger or sword?

Young Doreen was a tender child. She loved her mom and dad very much but living in the East End of London during the time of the Second World War was not easy. Sadly, her dad was an alcoholic, which meant there was no money for basic necessities. When she was 11-years old, Doreen's mom walked out on the family after her dad had an affair. The new woman in her life was very abusive and bullied Doreen and her sisters badly. Gradually, Doreen's esteem was stripped away. She found herself lost to the evils of witchcraft. But God had his hand on this young woman. Doreen eventually discovered that the love and supreme power of the holy Lord God Almighty, through Christ's blood, far outstripped any of the evil

141

power she'd found in Satan and witchcraft. She gave her life to Jesus. Repenting of her black crafts, Doreen Irvine became a woman sold out for Jesus. (You can read the story of Doreen Irvine in her book, *From Witchcraft to Christ*.)

Psalm 143 is a prayer of someone else who might have been bullied and abused – King David. As a young man, David was called by God and anointed as king of Israel. This happened while King Saul was still on the throne. Saul was not a nice guy and was not prepared to vacate his throne for this young upstart. Saul would attack David violently for no reason. David endured this abuse for many years, during which time he wrote many psalms. I call these the "Blues Psalms", because, in these, David pours out his woes to God. For instance, three times he writes, "Why are you downcast, O my soul? Why so disturbed within me?" but then always appends these words with the words, "Put your hope in God, for I will yet praise him, my Saviour and my God."

Perhaps you find yourself in a predicament similar to Doreen Irvine or King David. It could be that you are being bullied (or have been bullied) at home, at work or at school. It may be so bad that you fear the very thought of being anywhere near your abuser. This abuse may not necessarily be physical. Many people are verbally and emotionally abused to the extent that they can no longer face tomorrow. If that's you, then allow me to say to you, you are loved

– much loved! And you're not you alone. If you know and follow Jesus as Lord of your life, you are on the winning side! Listen: "Greater is he who lives in you than the one who lives in the world." Nothing can separate you from God's love, not even violent abuse.

If you're suffering abuse at this time, let me encourage you to not stand for it! Be courageous and seek godly help. The pain will only escalate if you keep it all to yourself. Then rest in your Lord's grace and his strength today. If your soul is downcast, call out for his comfort and sing with David, "I will yet praise him, my Saviour and my God." For his name's sake the Lord will preserve your life; in his righteousness, he will bring you out of trouble. Just trust in his love.

 **READ ALL ABOUT IT!**

Psalm 42:5 & 11 & 43:5; Psalm 143; 1 John 4:4 & 7-21; Romans 8:31-39

Pray

"Lord, you show me the way I should go because I lift up my soul to you. You save me from those who bully and abuse me. You are my hiding place. Help me to remain in your will, O Lord my God; your Holy Spirit leads my God-track on level ground. Preserve my life to the honour of your name and bring me out of trouble to your glory. Silence those who abuse me and those who deliberately cause me

143

pain. In your steadfast love you will cut off my enemies, and you will destroy all the adversaries of my soul, for I am your servant. Amen."

(Prayer Paraphrased from Psalm 143)

Week 37

GOD-TRACKING IS REVEALING GOD'S NATURE EVEN WHEN YOU'RE ABUSED

Proverbs 10:12

Hatred stirs up dissension, but love covers over all wrongs.

A story is told of a holy man who was engaged in his morning meditation under a tree whose roots stretched out over a riverbank. During his quiet time, he noticed the river was rising. A scorpion, caught in the trees' roots, was about to drown. He crawled out on the roots and reached down to free the scorpion, but every time he did so, the scorpion struck back at him. A passer-by said to the man, "Don't you know that it's in a scorpion's nature to want to sting?" To which the man replied, "That may well be, but I must change my nature to save, though the scorpion does not change its nature to sting."

So often we are confronted by people intent on our ruin, from those who simply contradict what we believe in, to those who abuse us just for the fun of it. But Jesus taught us to love our enemies and to do good to those who want to hurt us. Scripture also says that love covers a multitude of sins. This does not mean, of course, sin or abuse must be condoned. Rather, it means love demonstrates God's nature in all circumstances, despite the abuse. As God demonstrated his love for us in this, while we were yet sinners, Christ died for us. It's in God's nature to save!

If you are facing abuse or ridicule today, be encouraged to show God's nature to your abuser, even when they keep stinging you. If you are being contradicted or unjustly condemned, let me encourage you to walk in the proverbial opposite spirit and pray for those who wilfully hurt you. Remember, your fight is not against people but against the forces behind their actions – that is, Satan and his hordes.

So, stand strong, dear God-tracker, in the strength of God's love and might. Be sure to walk in truth while you wait on your Lord to renew your strength. Do not fret when people abuse you or ridicule your faith. Rather, be still before God as you wait patiently for his deliverance. Do not repay evil for evil but rather do good to those intent on hurting you. Remember, the Lord is your strength, your hope and your peace. He has an end in sight and his purposes will prevail.

⇒ **READ ALL ABOUT IT!**

Luke 6:27-36; 1 Peter 4:8; Romans 5:8; Ephesians 6:10-16;

Isaiah 40:28-30; Psalm 37:7-19; Romans 12:17

Pray

"Dear Father, I find I'm under attack again. I'm saddened because it's often the people I love who attack me. Help me to walk in the opposite spirit and not retaliate in the same way. Jesus, you taught me to love my enemies, so please help me to love these people with an unconditional love as your love for me is unconditional. I pray for them that you will heal their hurts and help them to come to know the freedom of walking with Jesus. Give me strength to get through this as I wait for your purposes to be revealed. In Jesus I pray. Amen."

Week 38

GOD-TRACKING IS SURRENDERING TO GOD IN PRAYER DURING LIFE'S BATTLES

Isaiah 40:29

He gives strength to the weary and increases the power of the weak.

The beginning of fear is the end of faith, but the beginning of true faith is the end of fear.

A story is told of how one of Napoleon's generals once appeared with 18,000 soldiers before a small defenceless Austrian town. The town council met and decided that surrender was the only option. However, the old dean of the church reminded the council that it was Easter and begged them to hold services as usual and to leave the trouble in God's hands. They followed his advice. The dean went to the church and rang the bells to announce the service. The French soldiers heard the church bells ring and concluded that the Austrian army had come to rescue the town. They broke camp, and before the bells had ceased ringing, vanished.

In this daily life we live as God-trackers, we are often faced with circumstances we deem beyond our control. Indeed, facing fearful situations well may be beyond *our* control, but if we are truly walking with God and acknowledging him in all our ways – in all our circumstances – then we can be sure God will direct the outcome of every situation no matter how "under" we believe we are. The Bible tells us God has made a way through every battle we face because of Jesus Christ's triumphed over our enemy at Calvary. Even strong people suffer anxiety and fret when circumstances get out of control. But those who hope in the Lord will renew their strength.

So, whatever difficulty you may be facing today first look for God's purposes before choosing any other option, and then believe he is in control. If you find your back is against the wall as you face financial strain, depression, bereavement and loss or physical illness, understand one thing: if you call on God before stepping out with that white flag, he will most certainly deliver you from the hand of your enemy. If you seek God first in your battle, every valley shall be raised and every mountain made low; rough ground shall be made level and rugged terrain will become a plain.

The next time you see armies massing on your doorstep, don't rush out with your hands up, instead go into your prayer closet and ring those bells of faith. Then take a step back and watch how God will rescue you from your fears!

⇨ **READ ALL ABOUT IT!**

Proverbs 3:5-6; Isaiah 40; Matthew 6:33; Colossians 2:15

Pray

"Dear God, when I look out the window of my life all I can see are armies massing against me from every side. I admit that I do not have the power in myself to stand against them. Lord, I need your help. I am feeling overwhelmed by my circumstances and realise that I need to seek first your righteousness and your kingdom. And so, dear God, I lay myself bare before you and call upon your strength to see me through. Lord, meet my needs, lift my spirits and heal my hurts. Lord, I claim your victory and blessing upon my life in the face of tis attack. I confess that Jesus has triumphed and, through faith in his name, I won't give up, I'll look up! I am more than a conqueror in Christ. Amen."

151

Week 39

GOD-TRACKING IS LOOKING THROUGH YOUR CROSS TO THE BLESSING BEYOND

Hebrews 12:2

... looking to Jesus, the founder and perfecter of our faith, who for the joy that was set before him endured the cross, despising the shame, and is seated at the right hand of the throne of God.

It was early hours of Friday morning and the night was very dark in the olive grove. Peter's eyes were heavy as he watched his Master from a short distance. He pulled his shawl higher to his neck as he laid his head back against an olive tree. He'd already had a short nap but now he watched as Jesus lay prostrate in the dust a few meters from him. Peter could hear what Jesus was saying. "*Abba*, Father," he said, "everything is possible for you. Take this cup from me. Yet not what I will, but what you will." Peter noticed that Jesus was very distraught. He'd never seen the Master this way before. What could it mean? Why did he come up here to pray at this hour? And then there were the things Jesus had said at the *Pesach*[a] *Seder*[b] earlier,

153

about the bread and the cup. Was this the "cup" he was now referring to in prayer? Peter's eyes blinked once, twice and he was asleep.

"Rise! Let us go! Here comes my betrayer!" Jesus' words startled Peter out of his slumber. A squad of temple guards with clubs and swords had entered the garden while Peter was asleep. Was that … yes, it was. Judas had just kissed Jesus' cheek and betrayed him to the temple guard! Peter drew his sword and lashed out at one of them, cutting off his ear. But Jesus, in his compassion, reached out and healed the man – his attacker – instructing Peter to put away his sword. They then led the one Peter had called the "Christ" off to be tried and executed. Peter followed at a distance.

Many years later, Peter sat chained in a small dungeon under the streets of Rome. He was an old man now and had been arrested by the Romans because he was the leader of the ones they called "Christians." He faced certain execution. In fact, Peter was eventually to be crucified just as his Lord had been, except he chose to be crucified upside-down. As he sat in his cell, his eyes grew heavy. His mind went back to that auspicious Friday morning in Gethsemane. Peter thought about how the all-knowing Son of God must have known all along that he would be arrested and sentenced to crucifixion. He could have arisen and gone down the hill back home at any time, yet he'd waited in the garden for his accusers to arrive. In the garden, Jesus was facing the cross. However, he scorned its shame, seeing himself beyond the cross, risen from the dead and seated beside Father God in glory. Peter then remembered the words once written in a letter address to the Hebrews, "Let us fix our eyes on Jesus, the author and perfecter of our faith, who for the joy set before him endured the cross, scorning its shame, and sat down at the right hand of the throne of God." Peter pulled up his shawl and laid his head back against the cold damp wall of his cell. His eyes blinked once, twice and he was asleep.

Dear friend, whatever you're facing tomorrow, take your eyes off of your difficulties and fix them on the Author of your life. Take his example, look beyond your needs and your problems and believe that Jesus is there already, on the other side of that wall, preparing your way forward. He is faithful and his love endures for you, forever. And then, for the joy set before you, endure your cross resting in his peace and victory.

 **READ ALL ABOUT IT!**
Mark 14:32-42; Hebrews 12:2-3

Pray

"Dear Lord, I'm sorry for getting so caught up in my problems. I realise now you are far bigger than any difficulties I may face and you are already on the other side of my tomorrow preparing the path

for me. I acknowledge you in all I am and all I do and choose to fix my eyes on Jesus, the author of my life. I scorn my cross and joyfully see myself uplifted on the other side of this pain. Help me to stand strong in the hope your Word gives me and help me to overcome these difficulties by your strength, for your glory. Amen."

---

[a] *Pesach* is the Hebrew word for Passover.

[b] *Seder* is the ceremonial dinner for the first two nights of Passover.

Week 40

GOD-TRACKING IS ACHIEVING TRUE HAPPINESS WALKING IN GOD'S WILL

Philippians 4:12

I know what it is to be in need, and I know what it is to have plenty. I have learned the secret of being content in any and every situation, whether well fed or hungry, whether living in plenty or in want.

In attempting to answer the question, "What is happiness?" pastor and author Clarence McCartney wrote, "Happiness is not found in pleasure. Lord Byron lived such a life if anyone did. But he wrote, 'The worm, the canker, and the grief are mine alone.' Happiness is not found in money either. Jay Gould, the American millionaire, had plenty of that. But when he was dying, he said, 'I suppose I am the most miserable man on earth.' Happiness is also not found in social position or fame. Lord Beaconsfield enjoyed more than his share of both. But he wrote, 'Youth is a mistake, manhood a struggle, and old age a regret.' Neither is it found in military glory. Alexander the Great conquered the known world in his day. But after having done

157

so, he wept in his tent and said, 'There are no more worlds to conquer.'"

So, what is happiness? I believe happiness is a state, not a strife. In other words, I believe happiness is not something we should strive for, but rather it's a state of mind that we automatically achieve as a consequence of our choices. As a disciple of Jesus, I believe true happiness comes from choosing to commit our lives to Christ and walking contentedly according to the will of God. I've discovered walking in God's will may not always be comfortable, but it will always bring peace, security and joy. Indeed, money can't make you happy; many friends can't make you happy; fame or status can't make you happy; and a life of pleasure can't make you happy. There is only one place in this world where true happiness can be found (irrespective of circumstances) and that place is in walking according to the prefect will of God.

The moment you said, "I do" to Jesus, you handed the pen of your life's story over to God. Your Heavenly Father knows your "then", your "now" and your "yet to be" – a knowledge too wonderful, too lofty for anyone to attain. Though it may sometimes seem that it's the end of the world as you know it, if you remain on track with God's will through Christ, deep within you will always have a true sense of peace, contentedness and *happiness*; a happiness that surpasses circumstance. So, wherever your life-track is leading you, continue to acknowledge God in all your ways and you'll happily walk according to his will.

⇨ READ ALL ABOUT IT!
Psalm 136; Philippians 4:10-13; 1 Timothy 6:6-10

Pray

"Dear God and Father, I know now there is no way to find true happiness in this life other than tracking in your perfect will, a track I find through the door of Jesus Christ. I happily confess and repent of all my sin and selfish desire to do things my may. I'm sorry for moving out of your will when things get tough. I now acknowledge you in all my life and make a choice to seek your will, always. Only through Jesus can I happily come in and go out, and find pasture, even in tough times. My happiness rests in this choice, O Lord: to walk joyfully where you lead me. So, I choose to not give up but look up, trusting you to direct my ways and keep me on the straight and narrow. Only in your will I find true happiness. Amen."

Week 41

GOD-TRACKING IS NOT HOLDING BACK WHEN GOD SAYS GO!

Isaiah 58:1
"Cry aloud; do not hold back; lift up your voice like a trumpet; declare to my people their transgression, to the house of Jacob their sins."

"Don't hold back!" These three words impacted me like a punch in the solar plexus. I was reading an email from a friend of mine whom I'd not seen in years. Bill had started out by wishing my family and me a happy Christmas, but his sentiment had turned from Christmas greeting to prophetic utterance: "Be bold and don't hold back. God is giving you a gift of faith. Use it or lose it." At the time, the Lord was leading us to plant a new church in our hometown. I was most encouraged by Bill's email, as I sensed the Lord leading us into new things and commanding us to enlarge the place of our tent, stretch our tent curtains wide and not *hold back*. With zeal I embarked on a programme of extending God's kingdom, declaring with the prophet Jeremiah, "His word is in my heart like a fire, a fire shut up in my bones. I am weary of holding it in; indeed, I cannot."

161

Two years after we started out, the Lord led us to unite with another small work to establish his purposes in our community. For several years we witnessed the growth of our new church as we saw people come to Christ and enjoy God's favour. However, I hasten to confess with embarrassment, I slowly became complacent in my zeal to preach, pray and prophesy. Somehow, I ended up simply going through the motions of church leadership, having lost that enthusiasm I enjoyed in the beginning. Sadly, I found myself holding back. I was learning the importance of being consistent in my obedience to the Lord's commands.

Perhaps God is doing a new and wonderful thing in your life, dear God Tracker. Your God is high and exalted. He is your Sovereign Majesty; his will is paramount; his character is supreme and his power unlimited. His plans for you are great and he will equip you to do his will by the zeal of the Holy Spirit and his Word. Today the Lord is filling you with a new-found stamina to prophesy his word, lay hands on the sick and be a witness to his authentic Kingdom Gospel. But remember, it's not by your prowess that you will accomplish his plans, it's only by God's powers that you will do so.

Be bold and don't hold back! Praise his name in the face of the gods of this world and stand up for the integrity of biblical principles in your community. You may think you're too weak to be this bold, but it's only when you admit your weaknesses that God empowers you to be stout-hearted by his grace. And his grace is enough!

Only by this grace have I returned to that passion the Lord gave me in the beginning. I continue to seek his strength that I may be consistent in all he has called me to be.

⇨ READ ALL ABOUT IT!
Isaiah 42:8-9; Isaiah 54:1-5; Jeremiah 20:9; Zephaniah 4:6; Psalm 138:1-3; 2 Corinthians 12:9

Pray

"O Lord my Majesty, forgive me for becoming complacent in my walk with you. I hear your Word afresh today, to not hold back; to be bold and courageous to stand by your principles in this society. Lord, help me to stand up in integrity and boldly profess your Word through my words and deeds. Help me to be brave in the face of the devil's opposition, knowing that my battle is not against people but against satanic forces in heavenly realms. So, I commit myself to you, as you work out your purposes in my life. Help me to fulfil your plans for me and not hold back! Amen."

Week 42

GOD-TRACKING IS TRUSTING GOD TO MEET YOUR NEEDS NOT YOUR MEANS

Matthew 6:8

...your Father knows what you need before you ask him.

I was made redundant from my job back in 2005. When it happened, I remember thinking how these things happen to other people, not me. But there I was – jobless. I was not earning a great deal at the time, but when that final paycheque ran out, things got really tough! My lovely wife was earning an income at the time, but it was just not sufficient to see us through each month. We prayed.

I was amazed as I watched our needs being met in the most awesome ways. We were most grateful to our dear friends who helped us – because they knew of our needs – but it was the times that we received provision from the most unexpected sources that we were totally blown away. Funny thing was, I was never able to tally up the numbers at the end of the month. It seemed God paid no attention to *how much money* we needed to get through the month, he was only concerned with *getting us through* the month. I am yet to reconcile the quantity of God's provision with the means he used to meet that provision. Somehow, we never had enough cash, but we always had enough provisions. God's ways are not our ways and his means not our means.

Don't be surprised, after seeking God's provision for a particular need, when he begins to provide in ways you would never have expected. For instance, you may be in financial need and receive an anonymous envelope. However, don't be disillusioned by a possible small amount you may find inside the envelope. The amount is immaterial; the mere fact that you received a material provision is paramount. God knows your needs – how *much* you need – and will always meet that need one way or another, provided you continue to keep your eyes on Jesus and walk by faith. Your God knows your needs and your God is wise enough to tally the numbers in order to meet those needs.

If you are a Christian believer, then you are found *in Christ* and the Bible says that God will meet all our needs according to his riches *in Christ*. You see, you are found in the same place as God's riches… *in Christ*! And your Father knows what you need before you even know how to pray. He has means beyond your wildest dreams!

⇨ **READ ALL ABOUT IT!**

Isaiah 55:8-13; Philippians 4:19; 2 Corinthians 1:19-20; Matthew 6:5-14

Pray

"My Father, thank you for always meeting my needs according to your glorious riches and wisdom. I realise that it's not how much *I need that matters, but rather it's* how *you provide my needs that does. You are my source and my resource. Not only are you the means of my provision but you are my provision! As I keep my eyes on Jesus, help me to walk in faith that you will meet all these needs I have, today. Help me not to question the means of your provision, but to just walk in the joy of your providence. I know you know how much I need to get through tomorrow, so today I simply put my faith in you to get me there. In the name of Jesus my Lord, I pray. Amen."*

Week 43

GOD-TRACKING IS MOVING FROM THE DRIED-UP BROOK TO THE WIDOW'S JAR, IN FAITH THAT HE WILL PROVIDE

Ephesians 3:20

Now to him who is able to do immeasurably more than all we ask or imagine, according to his power that is at work within us.

The Prophet Elijah sat on a rock in the Kerith Ravine. It was late afternoon and the sun beat down on him as he gazed at the dried-up stream bed. He lifted his eyes to the blue sky, but the ravens did not arrive that day. Elijah had followed the Lord's instructions to make his way to this spot after announcing a drought would hit Israel. Since then the Lord had kept him alive by sending the birds with meat and providing water by the stream. But now the trickle of water had stopped and the ravens were silent. Just then the Word of the Lord came to the prophet, "Go at once to Zarephath of Sidon and stay there. I have commanded a widow in that place to supply you with food." A widow? Elijah knew that widows were always poor and destitute. How will this work out? Rising, Elijah wrapped his cloak around him and started out for Zarephath. As he trudged along the dusty path, he might have wondered in his heart, "From a dried-

169

up brook to a widow's jar? I hope God knows what he is doing." You might say Elijah was going from the frying pan into the fire.

When he arrived at Zarephath, Elijah found the widow. She had a son. This poor woman was exceedingly destitute. The drought had stripped her of all possible means of feeding her son. In fact, she only had enough food left for one more meal for her son, how in the world was she ever going to feed the man of God? But the Word of God comes again to the prophet and Elijah announces her jar of flour will not be used up and her jug of oil will not run dry until the day the Lord gives rain on the land. And so, it was the widow and her son, as well as the prophet, enjoyed an endless supply of food according to the Word of the Lord.

You may be facing a drought today. It could be you feel like you're dropping from the frying pan into the fire. Perhaps you've been enjoying God's favour, but today you're facing redundancy or you've been disappointed by someone you trusted. If that's you, then know this: he who called you is faithful and will see you through the drought. He who began a good work in you will complete that work in his time and by his generous provision. Just as Elijah trusted God's provision when he moved from the dried-up stream to the widow's jar, so put your trust in the guidance of the Lord your God as you acknowledge him in all your ways. You can be sure that your jar will never run empty.

⇨ READ ALL ABOUT IT!

1 Kings 17; 1 Corinthians 1:4-9; Philippians 1:6;
Philippians 4:19

Pray

"O Lord, sometimes I feel as though I'm falling from the frying pan into the fire. Although things were not always ideal, I've known your blessings and provision but when I look at the future, somehow, I have no idea how I will ever make ends meet. But then I remember how you provided for your prophet Elijah when his resources dried up. Before you even led him into the unknown, you had planned his provision. Even though it was through a most obscure an illogical source, you cared for him and met his needs, as well as the needs of those around him. Thank you, Lord, that you have my life mapped out and that you will meet all my needs according to your wisdom and wealth. Today I put my trust in you and step out into tomorrow with confidence that you are there already, meeting my needs. Thank you, Lord. Amen."

Week 44

GOD-TRACKING IS OVERCOMING THE CANCER OF DEPRESSION BY THE HEALING POWER OF GOD'S WORD & PRAYER

Malachi 4:2

But for you who revere my name, the sun of righteousness will rise with healing in its wings. And you will go out and leap like calves released from the stall.

Jenni fell back against the wall on the balcony of her holiday apartment and slumped to her haunches, petrified and ashamed. It was early hours of the morning and while her husband Ed was asleep, she'd stepped out onto the balcony to get some air. She and Ed had taken a few days off to try and recoup their marriage. Jenni held down a high-powered job, but her career was collapsing. She and Ed were in deep financial debt and their marriage was crumbling. Jenni had nowhere to turn. She'd been keeping it all in; all those feelings of neglect, lack of self-worth and anxiety. She gazed back at the railing of their 11th-floor apartment's balcony. She'd come so close to ending it all.

Depression! It's safe to say that depression is becoming almost as common as the common cold these days. We're told that 10 times more people suffer from the disease today than 70 years ago. There are three primary levels of depression: mild, moderate and severe. A doctor will often prescribe drugs to deal with the symptoms of depression, but most doctors are now also suggesting "talking therapy." Talking out your problems is a very powerful form of treatment for depression.

The Bible makes it clear that everyone has a spirit, a soul and a body. The soul is your middleman – the part of you that links your spirit to your body. For the most part, your soul comprises your memories, reasoning and emotions. It is your soul that is mostly affected by depression. Your soul and your spirit are sometimes referred to as your heart. Now listen to what Jesus said about the heart: "For out of the overflow of the heart the mouth speaks." So, if you're suffering with anxiety and depression today, be encouraged to frequently pour out your heart to a faithful and compassionate confidant. However, there is another outlet for your confessions, which is probably more powerful than talking to a friend, and that is prayer. Prayer is also talking therapy. So, make a habit of daily talking to Jesus about your anxieties and problems.

Depression can often develop out of guilt, anxiety, sadness or low esteem. Everyone experiences emotions such as these from time to time, but it's when these types of emotions become malignant that depression sets into the soul. I call depression cancer of the soul. But cancer can be healed and Jesus is the healer! It was always by his Word that we see Jesus performing healings in the Bible. The Bible says that the Word of God is sharper than a double-edged sword. It penetrates even to dividing *soul and spirit.* Talking out your problems to God and a friend will begin the healing process, but the Word of God will complete it.

If you can relate to Jenni's story, and if you feel as though you're higher up and closer to the edge of your problems, then let me encourage you to pray and read the Word of God. Study the Word, confess the Word and live the Word. Allow it to penetrate and heal your soul. Here's an example of what God's Word is saying to you today …

O LORD, you have searched me and you know me. Before a word is on my tongue you know it completely, O LORD. You hem me in – behind and before; you have laid your hand upon me. Such knowledge is too wonderful for me, too lofty for me to attain. Where can I go from your Spirit? Where can I flee from your presence? If I say, "Surely the darkness will hide me and the light become night around me," even the darkness will not be dark to you; the night will shine like the day, for darkness is as light to you. For you created my inmost being; you knit me together in my mother's womb. I praise you because I am fearfully and wonderfully made; your works are wonderful; I know that full well. All the days ordained for me were written in your book before one of them came to be. How precious to me are your thoughts, O God! Search me, O God, and know my heart; test me and know my anxious thoughts. See if there is any offensive way in me and lead me in the way everlasting. [a]

If you're suffering depression, let me be quick to advise professional counsel. But never, never underestimate the power of prayer and reading the Word of God!

⇨ READ ALL ABOUT IT!
Luke 6:43-45; Hebrews 4:9-13; Psalm 119:105; Psalm 139

Pray

"Dear Lord, I believe I'm suffering depression. Help me to find its root cause and help me to root out its lies from my life and help me to find someone I can confide in. I confess I am a child of God and not a child of the father of lies. I reject Satan's lies in the name of Jesus. I confess Jesus as my Lord and master. I confess Christ

made a spectacle of depression when he triumphed over it at the cross. I confess that I need no longer be held captive under its icy grip. I confess to you that I seek to daily renew my mind by your Word. I believe you are familiar with all my ways; you hem me in behind and before; you have laid your hand upon me – your hand will guide me. You hold me fast. All the days ordained for me were written in your book before one of them came to be. Dear Lord, test me and know my anxious depressed thoughts and heal me of this cancer of my soul. In the name of my Lord Jesus, I make this my confession here today! Amen!"

---

[a] Psalm 139

Week 45

GOD-TRACKING IS CASTING YOUR CARES ON JESUS

Psalm 55:22 (NIV)

Cast your cares on the LORD and he will sustain you;
he will never let the righteous be shaken.

I am told that of all the issues an average person is anxious about, 40% of his worries are about things that will never happen; 30% are about the past that can't be changed; 12% are about the criticisms of others (mostly untrue) and 10% are about health issues, which get worse with stress! Of all the anxieties that he may suffer, the average person only worries 8% about real-life problems in any given day.

I went for a walk the other day with the cares of the world on my shoulders. I was anxious about many things: from cares about an ache in my knee to cares about other people in my life who were experiencing anxiety. As I walked, I prayed out loud for these needs (thankfully I was alone on a country path). I found myself complaining about mistakes I'd made in the past and what other people were saying about me in the present. The more I grumbled and worried, the tighter the knot became in my belly, until I almost audibly heard the voice of the Holy Spirit say, "Stop! Cast your cares upon me, because I care for you!" Immediately I stopped trudging that path and took out my mobile phone (it has a notepad app on it). I began to make a list of all that I was anxious about. Under a tree on the side of a hill in the English countryside that day, I did some *care-casting*!

Jesus told us not to worry about tomorrow. He told us to look at nature and see how God, in his perfect love and wisdom, takes care of the needs of the birds of the air and the flowers of the field. "Who of you by worrying can add a single hour to his life?" he said. "Therefore, do not worry about tomorrow, for tomorrow will worry about itself." Jesus then called us to be firstly concerned about God's kingdom and his righteousness. He promised that if we do this, all that we are worried about would simply fall into place. In other words, if you and I become concerned about the cares of this world, they will consume us and cloud our walk with God! However, if we seek first God's stuff in life, while casting our cares upon him, then we will enjoy his rest and reward. You see, God's kingdom is discovered through faith, and faith pleases God. Therefore, faith rewards the faithful who seek first God's purposes.

So, if you have the cares of the world on your shoulders, stop doing what you're doing right now and do some *care-casting*. Make a list of your worries and pray each of your needs through. Believe that the Lord, who is your strength and your shield, will meet all your needs according to his riches in Christ. Then make up your mind to seek first all that pleases God and step out in faith to believe that all these things you need in life will be added to you as well.

⇨ READ ALL ABOUT IT!
1 Peter 5:6-11; Matthew 6:25-34; Hebrews 11:6;
Psalm 28:6-9

Pray

"My Lord and God, I'm sorry for worrying so much. I realise that I have been consumed by the cares of this world instead of seeking first the things of your kingdom. Today, I lay down all my worries, cares and concerns at your feet. Dear God, today I do some care-casting in Jesus' name. I cast my cares on you – every financial need, every health concern, every worry about a loved one, every fear of what the future may hold and every offence that I have suffered at the criticisms of others. I do not give up, but I rather look up into your eyes for help and purpose. Thank you that you know my tomorrow and have a plan for my good future. Tonight, I will sleep in peace because you are my exceeding hope. Amen."

Week 46

GOD-TRACKING IS DAILY TRANSFORMING YOUR TOXIC THOUGHTS INTO GOOD NEW THOUGHTS BY HIS WORD

Psalm 25:8-9

Good and upright is the LORD; therefore, he instructs sinners in his ways. He guides the humble in what is right and teaches them his way.

I once listened to a talk by the cognitive neuroscientist Dr Caroline Leaf, who said, "Thoughts have substance. Thoughts occupy mental real estate. Your thoughts produce proteins, the body's building blocks, which form real structures that change the landscape of your brain!" She then described how we all have basically two types of thoughts and memories in our minds: healthy thoughts and toxic thoughts. She described how each brain neuron can be affected by proteins produced by stimuli that can result in either one or the other type of thought. Dr Leaf said that our brains have plasticity, that is, our thoughts can be shaped or changed at will. In a nutshell, she was implying that each one of us can harbour toxic thoughts or allow ourselves to remodel our toxic thoughts into good thoughts. We can change our behaviour and find relief from our fears and anxieties by renewing our thinking. But isn't this what was written about almost 2,000 years ago in the Bible, when it says, "be transformed by the renewing of your mind"?

So many of us suffer from depression and anxious thoughts these days that we're told that in Britain, for example, the prescription of anti-depressants has risen by 25% over the last 3 years. However, the Bible is clear that if we repent of sin, God, who is faithful and just, will forgive us and remove our sins from us. In other words, the Lord gives our spirits new life at the point of salvation – we become *new creations* when we accept the atoning work of Christ. This is what is understood by the term "being born again." You see, the Lord God loved you so much, even before you knew him, that he sent Jesus to die for your toxic thoughts and behaviour. When you asked Jesus into your life, he saved you through the washing of rebirth and renewal by the Holy Spirit. In Christ you *are* a *new creation*. However, your mind is still susceptible to toxic stimuli, resulting in toxic thoughts.

Therefore, daily and through prayer, you and I need to renew our minds by God's word and through the power of the Holy Spirit. If what Dr Caroline Leaf says is true, then science has proven we are able to change our way of thinking. It could be, for too long, you have allowed those toxic thoughts of guilt, sorrow, hurt or unforgiveness to cloud your mind. It may be that for years your thinking has been bunged up with worries, loneliness or low esteem. If so, today is the day to begin the process of renewal. Firstly, admit to and confess any known sin to the Lord. Secondly, pray and seek the power and grace of the Lord to help you overcome your problems. Thirdly, turn to his word and allow it to stimulate new and healthy thoughts in your mind. Do this by loudly confessing his truths over your life daily. Gradually, with persistence and perseverance, God's thoughts about you will become your thoughts about you.

⇨ READ ALL ABOUT IT!
Romans 12:1-2; Titus 3:1-7; 2 Corinthians 5:15-21

Pray

"Ah Sovereign Lord, you have made the earth and the stars by your word and the power of the Holy Spirit. Today I turn to you for that power to renew my thinking, by your Word. I confess that I have recently sinned – even in my thought life – and seek your forgiveness. I want to hold onto nothing that blocks the transformation of my old

toxic thoughts into new healthy ones. Help me to discover scriptures that will positively re-stimulate my thoughts and change depression into exaltation, for your glory. I begin today by confessing that in Christ I am a new creation, the old has gone and the new has come. Praise you for your love and goodness, O Lord. Amen."

Week 47

GOD-TRACKING IS REMAINING HOPEFUL IN SPITE OF HOPELESS PROSPECTS

Hebrews 10:23

Let us hold unswervingly to the hope we profess,

for he who promised is faithful.

Halford Luccock in his book *Unfinished Business* " tells this story: "One night at dinner a man, who had spent many summers in Maine, fascinated his companions by telling of his experiences in a little town named Flagstaff. The town was to be flooded, as part of a large lake for which a dam was being built. In the months before it was to be flooded, all improvements and repairs in the whole town were stopped. What was the use of painting a house if it were to be covered with water in six months? Why repair anything when the whole village was to be wiped out? So, week by week, the whole town became more and more bedraggled, more gone to seed, more woebegone." Then he added by way of explanation: "Where there is no faith in the future, there is no power in the present."

Hopelessness has a horrible habit of becoming increasingly hopeless the more one dwells on it. Many people are prone to a mood

187

of hopelessness. When they look at the glass, they see it as half-empty, always expecting the worst possible outcome to adverse circumstances. When difficulties come along – as they do in life – a hopeless attitude steps back in despair and takes its eyes off of the providence of Christ, while focussing on the problem rather than the solution. Sadly, a hopeless outlook will never enjoy the fruit of God's character-building in our lives, because hopelessness does not rejoice in challenge. Pessimistic hopelessness throws its hands in the air and gives up when things get tough. The scriptures tell us that suffering produces perseverance; perseverance, character; and character, *hope*. And Christ's hope will never disappoint us, because God loves us enough to take us through calamity and on into his wonderful plans, plans for a *hope and a future*.

Whatever emptiness you think your future may hold; whatever difficulty you're facing today or whatever loss you've endured in the past, I say to you never, never give up, only look up! God's Word has endured for millennia and you hold that Word right there in your hands. The Bible is crammed with God's positive promises to you. Listen: *God shall provide all your needs; the Lord is your Shepherd through the valley of the shadow of death; when you walk through the waters you shall not drown and when you walk through the fire you shall not burn; by his wounds you are healed; he has removed your sins from you as far as east is from west; God knows the plans he has to give you a hope and a future.* And all of God's promises are *yes* in Christ! So, if you are "in Christ," you are in the same place as God's promises!

Don't allow pessimistic hopelessness to bring your future into disrepair, even in the face of a bleak outcome. Live every day in the hope of God's newness and blessings. He who promised is faithful and he will do it!

⇨ READ ALL ABOUT IT!

Romans 5:1-11; Philippians 4:19; Psalm 23; 1 Pet 2:24;

Psalm 103:12; Jeremiah 29:11; 2 Corinthians 1:20

Pray

"Dear Lord, I'm sorry for my negative outlook on life. I want to change from a pessimist to an optimist. I reject this mood of hopelessness in my life and turn to you for overflowing hope for my future. You are my God and my Lord. You are my provider and my companion. Today I hand my future over to you and claim, by your Word, that you will meet all my needs according to your riches in glory in Christ. Lord, you are my hope for tomorrow. Amen."

---

[a] Luccock, H (1956). *Unfinished Business*. Harper & Brothers

189

Week 48

GOD-TRACKING IS SETTING OUR MINDS ON GOD'S SUPERNATURAL TRUTH

Colossians 3:2

Set your minds on things above, not on earthly things.

The traffic came to a sudden standstill. A man seemed to appear from nowhere. Suddenly the door of John's car was ripped open and a strong hand grabbed his arm, pulling him out onto the tarmac. "Get out! I want your car," said its voice. John scrambled to his feet in protest when suddenly there was a loud cracking noise. He slumped to the pavement. Spontaneously his hand grasped at his stomach. Blood seeped between his fingers. John had been shot by the carjacker who sped off in his car.

John lay in the intensive-care unit listening to a conversation between his father and a doctor. "You don't understand, Mr Kent, said the doctor. "The bullet missed his vital organs, but John's intestines have been ruptured. Their content has spilled out into his system. He will certainly become septic within the next few hours. It's touch and go. We'll need to monitor him every minute." The doctor was accurately describing John's condition, which was very serious, indeed. "No!" replied his father, "with all respect doctor, *you* don't understand. I have prayed for my son's safety and his healing. I believe that God will heal him. He will not become septic. I believe he will soon be home with us again."

God's Word is true and God's Word reveals God's will. Whatever the Bible says about life and living can be taken to be true for your life and mine. In the Bible it says that, in Christ, we have power to overcome the devil's schemes. The Bible also tells us that the devil is the father of lies, and in him there is no truth. But Jesus said, "I am the way the *truth* and the life." He also said, "I will do whatever you ask in my name." In Ephesians it says that, in Christ, we are seated in God's heavenly realms. Therefore, as we read in Colossians, we need to set our minds on *things above* and not earthly things. So when it comes to the comparison between natural evidence on earth and the fact of God's supernatural truth in the heavenly realms, I know which I'll believe.

John's father was not contradicting the physical evidence of the doctor's prognoses that night in the ICU. Rather, he was *choosing* to set his mind on things above and not earthly things. God's Word revealed God's will to heal his son and that's what he chose to believe. John slept peacefully that night while his temperature remained normal. He was discharged from hospital within 5 days and was well enough to travel a long hall flight within one week. God is faithful and his Word is true, always!

⇨ READ ALL ABOUT IT!

Luke 10:17-21; James 5:14-15; John 14:12-14;

Ephesians 2:4-10; John 8:44-45

Pray

"Holy God, thank you for your wonderful Word. Thank you that your Word reveals how mighty you are and how, in you, all things are possible. Today I make the choice between believing the natural evidence I see around me and believing the supernatural promises of your Word. I choose, therefore, to set my mind on things above and not earthly things by believing your Word. Dear God, I step out in faith and believe that you will bring about the answer to my prayers according to your revealed will. You are my healing, my provision, my guidance and my sustenance. In you alone I trust. Thank you, dear Father, for meeting all my needs. Amen."

Week 49

GOD-TRACKING IS TO KEEP MOVING ALONG YOUR JOURNEY OF LIFE, TOGETHER WITH YOUR GOD

Luke 9:62

Jesus replied, "No one who puts his hand to the plough and looks back is fit for service in the kingdom of God."

A few weeks back Karen and I decided to take a short break. We made plans to spend four days in a national park a short distance from our home. We set out early so we could stop off at places of interest along the way. No sooner had we encountered the motorway then we found ourselves in bumper-to-bumper traffic! The M6 motorway in the British West Midlands can be like a car park at the best of times, and this day was no exception. In fact, at one time we stopped for so long that the drivers around me turned off their engines and climbed out their cars. We'd come to a total standstill. Completely frustrated, I said, "I give up! If we really want to enjoy this journey, we need to keep moving!"

Many of us set off on the road to fulfil our God-given purposes with gusto but as soon as we experience congestion along life's highway and come to a standstill, we give up. Take the young woman who surrendered her life to Jesus at the Billy Graham campaign, for example. In the passion of the moment under the big top, she heard the gospel and put her faith in Jesus. Sadly, as soon as she hit the streets of the big city with its clutter and commotion, she drifted to a total spiritual standstill. And what about the middle-aged man who heard the prompting of the Holy Spirit to lay his career down in order go into the pastorate? Unfortunately, he procrastinated so long while *thinking about it* that he came to a dead stop in his faith-walk. You see, in order to journey along God's life-track for you, you need to keep moving.

Perhaps you find yourself at a spiritual standstill today. It could be you were once passionate about serving Christ but, sadly, the flame of zeal that set you ablaze has flickered and all but died out. Maybe you heard the call of God on your life several years back but the weeds of doubt, fear and procrastination have grown up and choked the life out of God's promises to you. Or it could be, like so many of us, you have simply become complacent in your faith-walk and find you're gaining no new ground in your journey with the Lord. Smith Wigglesworth said, "Live ready. If you must get ready when the opportunity comes your way, you are too late. Opportunity does not wait, not even when you pray. You must not have to *get* ready; you must *live* ready."

If you find yourself at a standstill on your life's journey, join me in taking the next exit from that backed-up highway. If you really want to enjoy this journey the Lord is taking you on, you need to put your foot down to keep moving.

 **READ ALL ABOUT IT!**
Matthew 13:1-23; Jeremiah 20:9; Luke 9:57-62

Pray

"Dear God, I realise today I have been procrastinating in my Christian walk. I know I've heard your call on my life but I've wasted too much time thinking about it instead of stepping out in faith to keep moving forward on the journey you have set before me. I'm sorry Lord. Today I re-commit my life to you and passionately seek to take your route for my future. I praise you for your love and your grace; grace that saves me and grace that equips me. I want to get going and keep moving on this journey you have set before me. I love you Lord. Amen."

Week 50

GOD-TRACKING IS A SYMPHONY OF PRAISE UNDER THE BATON OF THE GREAT CONDUCTOR

Psalm 104:33

I will sing to the LORD all my life; I will sing praise to my God as long as I live.

I remember day trips to symphony hall with school when I was a child. I loved listening to the music, but mostly I loved *watching* the full symphony orchestra playing so perfectly together. Dozens of musicians – brass, cords, percussion, wind – all playing as one. It seemed to my young mind as if they were all connected by a long invisible cord that moved their hands in complete unison. Then there was the guy up front with the wild hairstyle who waved a little stick around. The whole orchestra seemed completely mesmerized by his little dance while the invisible cord that connected their hands seemed to come from his baton and phenomenally flutter their fingers upon their instruments in a way that produced a vast array of

199

sweet sounds. They all seemed to be working *together* for the good of performing Vivaldi's *Four Seasons*.

Now, many years later, I still love symphony music, but at least I know now that the conductor does not have an invisible cord connected to each musician. And yet, I am still amazed at how every instrument works together with the other to produce beautiful music under his direction.

This reminds me of our walk with God. The scriptures tell us that all things work *together* for the good of those who love and serve Jesus. They also tell us that we are God's workmanship, created to do good works. Your life is an orchestra comprised of many intricate instruments that, in the hands of the Creator Conductor, will create marvelously melodious music. Every circumstance, every situation, every relationship and every activity you do, as acknowledging the Lord in it all, will work *together* symphonically for your good and his glory.

So, if you're finding yourself facing an inharmonic situation today, take your eyes off the musician to your left or right and fix them on Jesus, the great Conductor. Jesus is the author and perfecter of your life. He knows all you're going through and is already in your tomorrow, meeting your every need. If you will only allow him to conduct your life, his invisible cords will cause every detail to play in tune with his perfect will. He will turn your life into a masterpiece of his symphony. So, listen for his pitch and keep your eyes on your Conductor through every season of life.

⇒ READ ALL ABOUT IT!
Romans 8:28-39; Ephesians 2:8-10; Hebrews 12:1-3

Pray

"My dear Father and great Conductor of my life, I feel this word is for me today. Lately it seems as though the symphony of my life has gone out of tune. So I choose to acknowledge you again in every aspect of my life, from relationships to work; from pastimes to health and once again I put my trust in your hand to conduct the affairs of my life. Help me to serve you in harmony with those around me without comparing their performance to mine. Thank you that you meet my every need and conduct my every step. Thank you that you cause all things to work together in me – through all seasons of life – for my good and your glory. I take my eyes off my circumstances and fix them again on Jesus, composer and conductor of my life. Amen."

Week 51

GOD-TRACKING IS A LIFE SEASONED WITH THE POWER OF THE HOLY SPIRIT

Colossians 4:6

Let your conversation be always full of grace, seasoned with salt, so that you may know how to answer everyone.

I remember my first attempt at cooking a curry. Now, before I go any further, one thing you need to understand is, I'm no cook! Yet, with the counsel and direction of my talented wife, I once boldly attempted to cook up a dish fit for the Raj of India. The ingredients: sunflower oil, beef braising steak, onions, chopped tomatoes, garlic cloves, chillies, fresh root ginger, cumin, coriander, turmeric, garam masala, natural yoghurt and a handful of freshly chopped coriander. Hmm… I have to admit, it turned out quite okay.

I fully understand, not everyone who reads this thought may be a lover of Indian cuisine. However, I'm sure you'll agree that most of the ingredients listed above would make for a very fragrant and seasoned dish. Garlic, ginger, cumin, and coriander along with the others have strong flavours and fragrances. These herbs certainly influence the dish to produce its distinctive savour. However, if I were to remove these distinct ingredients, I'd be left with sunflower oil, beef braising steak, onions and chopped tomatoes. If I cooked only these components of the recipe without adding the fragrant spices and herbs, my splendid curry would have ended up nothing more than an average stew.

As we track the highways and byways of Christian living, we often find ourselves in situations that test the flavour of our faith. The scriptures tell us to make the most of every opportunity by allowing our interaction with the world to be seasoned as with salt. It says that we are the salt of the earth and the fragrance of Christ, which reveal God's flavour to the world around us. However, in my own strength I would find it impossible to reveal God's grace to my world. Though, when I allow my witness to be seasoned with the power of God's Word and Spirit, I become salt and light in a decaying and dark world. Jesus promised that the Holy Spirit would give us the words we need to speak when we're put on the spot. Therefore, make sure your conversation is always seasoned with the conscious presence of the Holy Spirit and his uncompromising Word. Only the seasoning of his Word and Spirit by grace and power can turn a humdrum stew into a fragrant offering fit for a king.

⇨ READ ALL ABOUT IT!
Colossians 4:5-6; 2 Corinthians 2:14-17; Matthew 5:13-16; Mark 13:10-11; John 16:13-15

Pray

"Heavenly Father, I realise that it is only by the fellowship and presence of your Holy Spirit in my life that will produce the seasoning I need to be your witness or be able to face conflict. You, O Lord by your Word and Spirit, are the salt of my being. Help me to rest in your inspiration and instruction as I interact with those around me. Only your power is the source of my strength; only Christ in me is the fragrance of life and only your grace is the source of all my ability. I surrender my conversations and interactions to you and seek your words when I'm called upon to share my faith. You, O Lord, are the essence that gives my life fragrance. Amen."

Week 52

GOD-TRACKING IS ENJOYING FULL LIFE IN CHRIST, TODAY

John 10:10 (KJV)

The thief cometh not, but for to steal, and to kill, and to destroy: I am come that they might have life, and that they might have it more abundantly.

Someone once said, "The tragedy of life is not that it ends so soon, but that we wait so long to begin it." So many of us (including the author) have great dreams and aspirations in life, but end up procrastinating so long that we become disillusioned and miss great opportunities.

But now is the hour! The Bible tells us that if we hear God's voice we need to respond today to enter his rest. Why then, after diligently committing our lives to Jesus, do we hold back on living out our new lives in Christ? Is it because we think Christians can't have fun? I believe Jesus did not only come to give us life *after* death, but he came to give us *abundant* life – life starting *now*! The Christian life begins when we enter God's rest the very moment we accept Christ as Lord, but it doesn't stop there. Christian living enjoys the rest of life in abundance from that moment on. And yes, even during trials and tribulations we can consider life to be pure joy.

Jesus is called "the Life." When Christ enters our hearts not only do we receive the promise of life *after* death, but we also gain the fullness of life *before* death. Living for Christ is no humdrum event. Living for Jesus is exciting, challenging and rewarding. We enjoy the rewards of God in this life by faith; those who track God's will by faith are rewarded by God. The Lord has plans of hope and a future for those who track his purposes by faith. God's plans will take us beyond our wildest imaginations. If it is true that Jesus gave us abundant life then let's step out in faith and take hold of those plans he has for us, today!

Perhaps you're a procrastinator, like me. If you are, then repent of it now and seek the Lord's help to realise God's exuberant plans for your life. The Christian walk is more than a set of religious rituals conducted once a week at church. The Christian walk is a lifestyle of worship to be celebrated every moment of every day. Tracking God's plans involves more than just Sunday morning kisses; it involves filling our daily lives with moments of intimate fellowship with *Abba* Father. God loves you so much and only desires the best for you; and nothing will separate you from his love. He has many new things lined up for you every day – every day is a new day that

God has made for you. Holy Spirit is omnipresent and omniscient. That is, he is personally with you right now, as he is with me, and he knows every little detail of your life.

So, dear God-tracker, take a step back from your hectic routine today and allow yourself to dream of great adventures and aspirations according to the plans your God has for you. Then step out in faith and enjoy your abundant life in Christ Jesus, today!

⇨ **READ ALL ABOUT IT!**
Jeremiah 29:11; Hebrews 4:7-13; John 4:6; James 1:2-4; Hebrews 11:6; Ephesians 3:20-21; Isaiah 43:18-19

Pray

"Dear Father God, thank you so much for the promise of eternal life that I have in you, through Jesus. I am so grateful for the life I will enjoy in the hereafter, but I'm also so grateful that the life you have given me, through Jesus, in the here and now. I commit all my life to you and acknowledge you in every aspect of my life: my relationships, my job, my church, my dreams and my ambitions. I praise you for abundant life and seek your plans for that life. Guide me in my aspirations and lead me in my desires that I may please you always. In faith, I claim your good plans for my future. Help me to walk according to your purposes, always. Amen."

Epilogue

So it is we have come to the end of another year of tracking the plans and purposes of God. The beauty of a book like this is, we can come back to it time and again for inspiration to continue to seek and track God's plans for our lives.

God-Tracking is based on the scripture found in Proverbs three that reminds us to acknowledge God in all our ways. If we do so, then we can be confident that he will direct the paths – the tracks – of our daily lives. Therefore, the secret in remaining on track with God's plans is to continue to acknowledge God in *all* our paths, every day. My encouragement to you then is to make a conscious commitment to seek and track God's will by daily acknowledging him through prayer and confession.

Our God is high and exalted. He is our Sovereign Majesty, his will is paramount, his character is supreme and his power unlimited. I pray our Lord will continue to bless and guide you as you keep your eyes on him.

Thank you for reading God-Tracking Through the Year – year two. I pray it has been beneficial to your walk with God.

Dudley Anderson

About the Author

Born and raised in Johannesburg, South Africa Dudley Anderson began writing for radio in 1994. In 1997 he moved to the UK where he joined an international Christian radio station, reaching millions of people across central-southern Africa on short-wave and FM. Since 2005 he has freelanced on several Christian radio stations in the UK and produces programme material for many stations around the world.

Dudley currently writes a weekly e-mail Christian motivational though called GodTracker, which developed as an offshoot of a radio show he produced called, On-Track. On-Track was heard by millions of people across Africa. This e-mail motivational thought has been running since July 2003 and reaches hundreds of people worldwide. GodTracker is published online via the website www.surereality.net

Find out more about tracking the plans and purposes of God for your life by subscribing to the free e-mail Christian motivational thought, GodTracker at www.surereality.net

To contact Dudley Anderson e-mail dudley@surereality.net

For more information about GodTracker scan the Q.R. code below or visit www.surereality.net

Printed in Great Britain
by Amazon